Faith and Fear
to
Faith Over Fear

by Mary Lou Moreno B.Ed./M.Ed.

DORRANCE
PUBLISHING CO
EST. 1920
PITTSBURGH, PENNSYLVANIA 15238

Dorrance Publishing Co
585 Alpha Drive
Pittsburgh, PA 15238
Visit our website at *www.dorrancebookstore.com*

ISBN: 979-8-8868-3257-0
eISBN: 979-8-8868-3653-0

From the time I was three years old, I first experienced racism and prejudice. I didn't know what it was at the time, I only knew that there were differences in people. I began to notice differences in individual attitudes, customs, and beliefs at a very early age. The differences in the color of people's skin caused them to be looked at and thought of as different. At the time, I didn't know about different races and certainly didn't know the meaning of prejudice or being prejudged. As a three-year-old, I had no idea about the origins of people, where they originated from, and what brought them to America. As a three-year-old, how was I to know that Spanish/Mexican folkways would still shape the lives of countless Americans so many decades later? I didn't know a thing about civil war and much less civil disobedience. I had no clue until a study of my grandfather Leon Perez and his father's background has been studied and discovered that that particular Perez family was among the families who founded Albuquerque, New Mexico. It was during my early childhood days that I listened to my grandmother Antonia tell us some legends, folktales, humorous tales, and, my favorite, cautionary tales. These stories were told over and over and I never tired of listening to them. My early childhood days were filled with the sheer enjoyment of listening to adults tell their stories, listening to my parents and grandparents reminisce about the stories that had been told to them by their parents and grandparents. Little did I realize that word-of-mouth learning experiences and celebration of traditions would shape the world in which I was a part of. My mother would also tell us these stories by memory. They were not only bedtime stories, but stories that she related to us to teach us a lesson on obedience and being cautious in different situations. At times, I felt that our parents and grandparents were overly cautious about teaching us safety. It wasn't until many years later, that I learned to appreciate what they were trying to teach us. The advice they gave us made much more sense as a teenager and as an adult than as a young child.

1 As a toddler in Munday, Knox County Texas, I lived with my parents, two brothers, and two sisters on the outskirts of town. Across the railroad tracks. I didn't realize I was poor or that we lived in the "poor" part of town. It wasn't until many years later that I realized that we didn't have any luxuries. I didn't know the difference. I just knew that the part of town in which we lived the houses weren't as big and beautiful like others in other neighborhoods. I assumed then that we lived in a regular part of town. I knew nothing about living in the "poor" part of town. I assumed that all people lived like us. Later in life, I learned that children learn from adults the difference between being poor and living a full life with few resources. My maternal grandfather Leon Perez, along with my maternal grandmother Antonia Sandoval Perez and several of my aunts and uncles lived on a few acres in a row of houses east of town. The houses were small but quite adequate for our families. The grounds had areas of grass and had blackberry trees where

my siblings and I along with a host of cousins roamed freely. The older children went to school along with other Hispanics and Anglos on the opposite side of town. It was at a time when all children walked to school unless they lived far out in the country. Being the youngest of five in my immediate family, I stayed home with my other toddler cousins, my mother, and grandmother. Children old enough to go to Munday Elementary, junior high, and high school walked the twelve or thirteen blocks to school. Few of the older children stayed in school long enough to graduate. They were expected to help in the fields after school. At a very early age, we learned about cooperation, contributing to helping out with chores, and obedience. My grandfather, my dad, and my uncles worked in the fields, the gin or the vegetable warehouses as the little town of Munday was known as the "Vegetable Capital of the World". Watermelons and cantaloupes were plentiful as well. Often times the aunts joined the uncles in the fields, plowing, planting, chopping cotton, picking cotton, or collecting vegetables from the fields. With cotton ginning season lasting well into the winter months, field work was plentiful for at least ten of the twelve months of the year. Compress and vegetable warehouse work employed most of the migrant families in the small community. Everyone in the families helped in the canning of food for the winter and stockpiled the food in the cellars. There were two large cellars the families shared. Women in the family regularly made the clothing for the family. Material was often hard to come by, so the women would use the cloth in which flour was sold. Not only did they make dresses, skirts, and shirts, but also pillowcases and rags for cleaning. Parents would also be in charge of cutting the children's hair as no barber shop in town allowed Mexicans or Blacks to use their facilities. For a long time, I was unaware that the barbershops in town didn't allow Blacks or Mexicans to use their services. During these years, I would daily watch the Black children come across the tracks walking in groups toward their own school, the school for Negros only. What could a three-year-old possibly know about Brown vs Board of Education? I had no knowledge of segregation and de-segregation. Mexican-American and Anglo children attended the same school, separate from the Blacks. Mexican-American was a term used to describe children of Mexican descent but during my childhood we were only called Mexicans. Watching the Black children go to the "Negro School" raised questions in my young mind. Why didn't all children attend the same school? Was it because their skin color and hair were different? Why were they separated to attend their own school? Why were all the teachers white? Why were the Black children not allowed to stop and talk to the Mexicans? Black families also lived in a separate part of town. They were instructed to move quickly through the "row of Mexican houses". I now believe those Black children were as scared of mixing with the Mexican children as we were of mixing with them. Fear is also a factor that is sometimes the cause of mis-understanding. Fear of the unknown or the unfamiliar takes people out of their comfort zone and in turn people jump into making false assumptions. Meanwhile, the Mexican students in the regular school were instructed to eat in a certain area of the cafeteria as to not mix with the Anglo children. Even in the playground during recess, Mexican children had to only play with other Mexican children. They were forbidden to play with the Anglo/white children. My siblings would question our parents, our aunts, uncles, and grandparents as to why they were kept separate from the white children in the classroom as well as in the cafeteria. Minimal contact was tolerated in the playground. Mexican children always expressed a sense of relief when they returned to the security of their home and families after school. Being in familiar territory gave them a sense of security, acceptance, fitting in, and being included are things that all human beings desire. We, the toddlers, lived a carefree happy-go-lucky life of playing tag, making mud pies, climbing trees, and rolling down the hills of dirt which were like a mountain (hill of dirt that covered the huge cellars on our properties). If we ever suffered a fall, a scraped knee, or other minor injury, our grandparents would recite to us, "sana sana colita de rana, si no sana mañana, sana la otra semana" or would tell us "Pajarito, Pajarito" sort of equivalent to "Look at the birdie" to distract us from feeling sorry for ourselves for the minor injury.

All of us "Mexicans" would participate in "curar de susto" (curing a child who had suffered a tremendous frightful experience) and "el mal de ojo" (the evil eye) which caused a child to have fever and nausea) which were rituals performed on us especially by our grandmothers who passed these rituals on to their children and grandchildren and to this day are practiced in many Hispanic families. Even though Spanish-Americans and Mexican-Americans claim to be different, some of the customs and traditions have roots in the mixture of these cultures. Spanish/Mexican folklore, songs and rituals share a commonality that has lingered for centuries. Some of these rituals have nothing to do with actual darkness and evil nor associated with any religious exorcism and practices. One expression that parents used to put the fear of God in their children was "el cucuy" (the evil one) (the devil). However, we only thought of "el cucuy" much like the way Anglo children were threatened with "the boogie man". We children never thought of "el cucuy" as the "real" devil but sort of as "you better listen or one of your parents would come in and spank you or take a privilege away". We, children of every age, enjoyed picking blackberries after being told to steer clear of the blackberry trees as our mothers would be along to pick the blackberries and prepare them to make jelly or pies. A childhood where a child is loved unconditionally by two Christian, God-fearing people who absolutely never mentioned a word about people not being equal was enjoyed by all of us at an early age.

2 No one ever seemed to take offense at being called a Negro, a Mexican, or a Gringo (a common, courteous, yet slightly derogatory term for Anglos and a "greaser" for Mexicans). However, if one Mexican called another Mexican "agringado", a term of contempt, meant that he was getting to "yankee-fied". Another term I often heard older Hispanics call one another was "Tio Tomas" Uncle Tom meaning that that particular person was taking the side of his "patrones" or other Anglos at the expense of his own kind. I knew nothing about what people are now calling "white privilege". In high school, I often heard Hispanics call others "Oreos" meaning they were "brown" on the outside and "white" on the inside. Ethnic labels, as far as I'm concerned, have a long history of existence and will always be around. Children learn what they hear and eventually these adages become part of their vocabulary. Some people will literally take offense at these and others will not. I never knew anyone to take offence to these names while I was

growing up. I remember the common term of "cholo" used to describe people of low class in their culture to "cholo" being used as an endearment to describe a young person who is proud of where he comes from. Often times a play on words was so common that it seemed as a third language was developed to communicate with certain groups. Sayings among Hispanic teen agers was quite common in our neighborhood. Yes, even in small towns such as Munday, Texas and Tulia, Texas. I would hear them use such made up terms as "de aquellas" meaning very nice and "estaba en el bote" - meaning he was in jail (bote meaning can). The word "huevos" literally meaning eggs – has a part in this play on word such as teenagers saying "huevon" to mean lazy and "no tienes los huevos" – meaning you don't have the guts (balls).

It wasn't until I was in college that I began to hear that it was only acceptable to say African-American, Latino, Hispanic, Mexican-American, and Anglo. The Chicano movement arose at about that time. I always wondered why they got rid of their ethnic designation as Irish, German, and Scottish, yet when asked about their ancestors they would proudly say and to this day still proudly say, "I'm Irish, Russian, German or French or Italian". I always wondered, if they were part German, Russian, Irish, French or Italian, why did they not keep their ancestor's part of their language? I learned much later from a lady of German origin that their parents told them it was much safer to forget their German language and assimilate completely to the English language. They were also prejudged but chose not to go against the grain and assimilate language and all to this country's customs and adhere to what was considered "acceptable". Now in her late eighties, she has told me that she now considers it was a mistake to let go of her German language. She married a man of Italian descent and they too let go of their Italian language. Even though some of their old customs and beliefs are of German and Italian origin, they still practice them to this day.

I'm always amazed how people find foreign accents such as British, Italian, and others fascinating, yet a Spanish speaking person speaking English sounds repulsive to some. I have found in my travels all over the world that people from different countries will bend over backwards to help you understand their language and cultures, yet we as English speakers expect others to speak English. We ridicule foreigners who come to America and speak broken English. I dare to say, that when traveling in a foreign country, we speak their language brokenly as well. People from other Spanish speaking countries such as Costa Rica and Honduras have a heavy accent when speaking English, yet they are not ridiculed as much as a person of Mexican descent having a heavy Spanish accent. I have heard so many people say street signs, hospital signs, and any other public signs should only be in English. They should not be in Spanish. People should learn to function in English. I agree, people in the United States should aspire to master the English language, but if you are an English, monolingual, don't take offense to these things, use them as learning tools to help you acquire some "foreign" language skills yourself. Try learning a new language. You will find it refreshing and you will be a much better traveler in this increasingly shrinking world.

Mexican-Americans and Anglos went to the same school, but the Blacks had their own school. I remember one tradition in particular where Mexican people would hang a pair of baby shoes from the rearview mirror to announce the arrival of a baby to the family. For a Spanish family, it was considered taboo because it could mean that a baby would soon die or be in a car accident. We loved to aggravate another set of elderly grandparents that lived on the premises. Those grandparents were related to some of our cousins on their dad's side of the family who also had a house in that row of houses. Even with our elderly grandparents, we would have fun with our play on words. Sometimes we would even laugh when people transposed the "Sh" and "Ch" until much later learning that in the Spanish language – they are interchangeable. In this day and age, I still see people ridicule Mexicans who say "shurch" for church or "shair" for chair. I just chalk it up to their lack of knowledge of the pronunciation of such words in the Spanish language. I don't get defensive because it only causes me to have to go into a detailed explanation of why it is not the end of the world to pronounce such words "incorrectly". We did, however, at a young age learn that the employers of all the working people in our family were white/Anglo. Our grandfather, dad, and other extended members of our families were very loyal to the "patrones" (the bosses and their wives). Therefore, we learned loyalty, faithfulness, and respect for authority. Was this "white privilege"

I was being exposed to at an early age or was I merely being taught respect for elders? At this point in my life, I had no clue why the Mexican men and women were not "patrones" ever. They were always the hired hands, the minimum wage earners, never the landowners or the bosses. Family was considered the most important part of our lives. I remember when my older brother leased some land south of town (Tulia) in the late '60s, I would hear people say, "Well, he doesn't own the land, he is just leasing it." SO? He was the boss of that land and the workers he hired. No white person wanted to have a Mexican boss. They felt that that was beneath them and were openly vocal about that feeling. Where did that feeling come from? As a result, my brother had only Mexican and Black farm hands. We learned that our parents were in charge of our upbringing and the respect we showed our elders and the "patrones" was unmatched. In Knox County, we came to love two families that were "patrones" - The Myers and the Urbanczyk families. Even though they were the "boss" they treated everyone with dignity and respect. Living a carefree life as a young child was the only life I knew. Little did I know I would embark on a whole different set of rules, values, and ways of seeing the world as a pre-teen, a teenager, a young adult, and in my adult life. Seeing the cultural differences in belief and customs, we can come to the conclusion that we all may do certain things or observe different traditions which are basically the same but may mean different things to different groups of people. I had no idea Mexican/Indian/Spanish folklore would shape the traditions and customs I would learn as a child and carry on into adulthood.

I often think of sayings that can't be literally translated from one language to another but have basically the same meaning. For example: To be "entre la espada y la pared" which literally translates to "between the sword and the wall" but has the same meaning as when in Texas we say "between a rock and a hard place". I absolutely loved my childhood years. The innocence and happy-go-lucky type of childhood is missing from our society today. I see many children totally taken over by the likes of cellphones, iPads, tablets, and other forms of technology readily available to today's youngsters. While technology is totally necessary this day and age, I often think it is misused by young parents to take the place of a babysitter or they themselves giving time to their children. It is rather disheartening to see a young parent on the phone, oblivious to what their children are doing and showing great signs of annoyance when their children ask them questions. This is another example of children learning from their role models to dismiss the curiosity of others, that hunger to gain knowledge, those intriguing questions going unanswered. I see them at times hand the child a phone or tablet to settle them down or to keep from being bothered by their questions. Proverbs, riddles, rhymes, and folklore are losing their place in our lives today. Technology is totally acceptable and necessary in today's world, but much is lost by googling everything and not using the brain we were given to figure things out in our head, to do the math in our head, and to problem solve and reason on our own. In some instances, we would be lost without the technology that is available to us today.

We are living in a new era, in the time of the pandemic of the coronavirus, which has crippled many nations around the world. Homes and computers and "zoom" conferencing have become the norm. Parents have become the teachers of their own children in their makeshift classroom, a.k.a. the kitchen table. Much frustration has overtaken not only the parents, but the entire school system. Teachers have had to adjust to teaching in a completely different setting from the traditional classroom.

As in the days of peaceful protests led by Dr. Martin Luther King, we are seeing protests all over the world again in the wake of the death of George Floyd who was killed by a police officer while others stood by and watched. Some even recorded this dreadful incident. There are many injustices in the world, as there always have been. I have no respect for those who break the law as well as for those who abuse their power. I have a soft place in my heart for peace officers who risk their lives daily for our protection. We have lofty expectations of our police officers and expect them to be at our beck and call when needed. We want their protection and service, yet we forget that they too are normal people who have a family with needs. They too deserve our respect. One bad apple spoils the whole barrel in any line of work, be it law enforcement or any other profession. Just as not all people who go to jail are terrible no-good scoundrels, not all police officers are murderers and worthless. The search for justice has taken on a completely new twist. Calls to defund the police seem rather harsh. We want the police to be there when we need them. We have lofty expectations of our law enforcement officers and first responders, yet many fail to understand the gravity of not being supportive of those who tend to emergencies and the well-being of communities in general. Children learn what they live. If a parent or adult in a child's life disrespects authority, the children may follow that path of disrespect for authority. Again, children practicing what has been modeled to them.

Communication with today's technology would be impossible without the ability for instantaneous means of communication. During my childhood years, adults respected us as much as we respected them. I am saddened by the lack of respect for property and objects that represent our history such as the statues that are being torn down. Many people who have been interviewed about the destruction and tearing down of confederate symbolism really had no idea why they were wanting the statues down, but were followers to those who were leading the pack in search for "justice". How is justice being accomplished by destruction of property and killing of individuals? I often wonder why we have such protestors in great numbers for a long period of time. Do they not work? In my young life, I had never heard of organized crime. Later in life, I have learned that this really does exist. Where did organized crime develop? Where did it come from? Again, youngsters learned this from the adults around them and the media.

Where do these rioters get the money to keep their households going and paying their bills if they are continuously rioting and protesting? Are they being funded by individuals and corporations that want the violence and commotion to continue? Church was a very important part of our life. We developed many necessary skills by going to church. We learned to read the Bible, hymnals, and do public speaking. Those skills have become such a valuable part of who we grow up to be. People don't seem to want to talk things out anymore. Texting has become the norm. Even youngsters who looked for their parents for guidance and advice are now googling for the answers and/or texting their siblings instead of holding a conversation with them. Our grandparents and parents would have a word or two about that behavior! One specific behavior I have to share where customs and beliefs differ became quite evident to me growing up was when an adult was correcting a child (in Hispanic culture) we were expected to look down (a show of respect). In Anglo culture, when an adult was correcting a child, they often used the phrase, "Look at me when I am talking to you." These two cultural differences have caused many Hispanic children in this culture to have a conflict as to what is the right way to behave in certain situations when one is being corrected. I quickly learned, as my siblings and young relatives did, that when we were at home and being corrected by an adult, we looked down and when we were in school and being corrected by the teacher, we learned to looked her "in the eye". Some children had a harder time than others learning to make the switch in these situations.

We learned a lot about God and his infinite love for us, about his grace and about obedience to the laws of God, our parents and all our extended family. I have nothing against anyone worshiping in their own religion or sect. After all, freedom of religion is in our constitution. I should have no say in how anyone worships as I feel no one should have a say in how I worship. Sometimes I get offended when ridiculed about some of my religious practices, but I have to be the bigger person and chalk it up to ignorance on their part. As long as I know and believe in our Lord Jesus Christ, I merely shake it off and move on. As a young child, I remember even holding funeral services for our pets. I learned many years later that even in a cemetery there are divisions. My experiences are with Johnson Cemetery in Munday and Rose Hill Cemetery in Tulia. There are divisions. The Mexicans are mostly buried on the North side and the Blacks are buried on the Northwest side. Some Hispanics are sprinkled among the graves mostly occupied by the Anglos. What a morbid sight. Even in death, on this earth, we continue to make divisions. Surely in heaven we will not be divided. Will we have a choice in what part of heaven our mansion will be located? My niece and I would dig the grave and then argue as to which one of us would preach and which one of us would sing at the pet funeral. One of my favorite cautionary tales or custom was "The Wake", "El Velorio". We could relate because during my childhood days, it was customary for the deceased person's body to be brought to the home of that person. The adults would stay up and visit, pray, and tell stories of that person's life. We as children would sometimes listen in on their conversations but were not expected to take part in the "velorio". I remember the women would gather in the kitchen preparing food or storing food that the townspeople would bring to the house of the deceased. As children, I remember playing outside with the other children, but we weren't our usual rowdy selves. Our parents expected us to be respectful so we played games that weren't too rambunctious. The teenagers wanted nothing to do with us toddlers so they separated themselves and visited with all other teenagers whose parents came to the "wake". Sometimes we would hear the adults praying, reading scripture, and singing softly. I thought it was a little eerie but never did I think of criticizing what rituals they practiced. I only remember the "velorios" of my uncle Joe, my aunt Cesaria who lived in Olton, and my uncle Andres – el Grande in Tulia. I knew other Hispanic people had this custom but my parents rarely took us along with them to other "wakes". I never remember any Anglos or Blacks at any of these "velorios" so I just assumed it was a Hispanic custom and tradition. We experienced very little negative drama in our young sheltered lives. Our parents, grandparents, aunts, uncles, and cousins would gladly join in family fun of "cuentos" (stories, folklore) songs, games, and customs of our ancestors.

Just shortly after my fourth birthday, our extended family began to scatter to follow the seasonal crops. My grandparents' family of thirteen was beginning to change. All the younger aunts and uncles were getting married and forming their own families and homes. All of us who until at that time had been living in that row of homes across the tracks, children being born at home with midwives "parteras" (midwives) was coming to a close. We left the comfort of that familiar neighborhood in Munday, Texas to move to Chicago so my parents and older siblings could work in the tomato fields.

My imagination was quickly developing as I had to entertain myself. I sang the old songs taught to me by my parents. I particularly remember "Uno de Enero, dos de Febrero" that was used by my parents to teach us the numbers as well as the months of the year. Many years later, I taught my beginning Spanish classes the same song to teach them the numbers and months in Spanish. Years later, some of my former students say they still remember those "old teaching songs" from Spanish classes either in elementary or high school. The days were long with long working hours. Everyone had a designated job in the tomato fields. Mine was carrying water to the field workers, my sister's job was carrying small and large baskets to the workers to fill. My sister and I, who were too young to be paid employees, had to entertain ourselves. We had to make do with what we could find. The long hours at the edge of the tomato fields served as a playground for us children. I remember playing childhood games such "A la vibora de la mar", a variation of "London Bridge". To decide who was to do what, we would use the "pin marin de Don Pingue, cucara, macara, titere fue", basically "Eeny, Meeny, Miny Mo". These two ways of designating the chosen one was quite common. The highlight of my summers in Chicago was that on Saturday afternoon my parents would take us to a place called "Kiddy Land," which was an amusement park. The merry-go-round fascinated me with its lights, beautifully decorated horses, and music. I would let my imagination run wild. The sounds of laughter and the smell of cotton candy and popcorn were the best. The laughter and joy I shared with my parents and siblings were so much fun. My favorite things to eat were corn dogs and snow cones (not shaved ice)! I can still taste the strawberry flavor and the crunchy ice. My brothers liked to play the games such as dart throwing and bb gun shooting. They won toys and my sister and I were elated. They loved to ride the Ferris wheel and the tilt-a-whirl. Saturdays were such fun family times. Sunday was a church day.

We played in the ditches of the fields playing with metal cars, building bridges with dirt, sticks, and rocks, and being creative with bottle caps from the glass bottles as we had no canned sodas or plastic bottles. We all drank water from five-gallon cans and a dipper. We were careful not to break the bottles as they were good for the deposit we would get in return. One memory that I have of breaking a bottle was when my sister taught me a game which had the jingle – "Down by the river, down by the sea, Johnny broke a bottle and blamed it on me. I told Ma, Ma told Pa. Johnny got a whipping and a, 'Hahaha!'" I didn't get a whipping, but a forty-five minute lecture from my dad on the dangers of breaking bottles. I learned. I remembered we collected bottles to take to the grocery store to earn a deposit refund.

We stayed in the Chicago area till the tomato season came to an end. My father secured a job in Dimmit, Texas for one year. There our parents worked in the sugar beet, onion, and potato fields. Planting, caring for, and harvesting these vegetables was commonplace. Factories were built in Dimmit to make necessary sugar from the beets and to carry the potatoes to the potato warehouses in nearby Hart, Texas. The following year, we moved to Tulia where my father found work. During this time was when my oldest sister moved to Isleta, Texas to attend Latin American Bible Institute. I was very young, but I remember making the trips to El Paso to go visit my sister in Bible school. In those days, there were no infant seats, no seat belts, etc. I remember sleeping by the rear window, enjoying the warm sun. We packed our lunch and would stop at a roadside park to eat. Few restaurants along our way allowed Mexicans to enter. They were not timid about posting signs letting us know we were not allowed in their establishments. We took it all in stride and just carried on. We simply abided by the regulations imposed on us. Causing trouble and being rebel rousers was not on our agenda. My brothers would ride in the front seat of the car with my father, taking turns driving. My sister and I rode in the back seat, which resembled a large couch. We would sing, read, and argue of course. We played games with the brands of cars, be they a Chevrolet or a Ford, etc. That was when there were not so many makes and models of cars.

My two brothers were eight and ten years older than me so to them I was somewhat of a nuisance. I went through the stages of tattling on them if they even thought of uttering any profane words or chasing me or giving me a hard time. I learned very early about loyalty and gossip. My parents would absolutely not tolerate gossip. If I accused my brothers of a wrongdoing, I better well have proof. These trips went on for as long as my sister was in Bible school. A few years later, she graduated with a certification in Biblical studies. Shortly upon her return from Bible school, she married a hometown boy who also graduated from the same Bible school. Her husband became a pastor of a church. They moved around quite a bit, be it Texas or Oklahoma. The ministry took them to several towns. Some of my aunts and uncles moved to California to pick cherries or strawberries, others left to Florida to work in the citrus fruit seasonal work, others moved to Idaho to work in the potato fields and warehouses. Others joined the military. Others moved to other parts of Texas. My brother and some of our cousins even ventured up to Minnesota is search of seasonal work. They were quite young but made their way in other states. We were migrants, as our families moved to follow the crops. We learned much about cotton, vegetables, fruits, sugar beets, potatoes, and wheat. We were raised around tractors, combines, irrigation ditches, cotton picking, chopping cotton, etc. I am saddened to watch the news where vegetable farmers are having entire fields go to waste because there is no one that wants that menial job of harvesting the crops. They tell of the farm laborers from Mexico and other south and central America who can no longer come to work because of the border being closed to them. It is sad that those who need the work and those who can provide the work are separated by governmental regulations that prohibit this exchange of labor practices.

I experienced working in the fields with many crews. The most vivid crews in my memory are the crews of Chavela and Waldo Galán who secured work in the fields with Taylor-Evens Farms, Abdon Rodriguez Sr., and Victor Cardona. It was working in the cotton fields that I learned much about the "old days" working alongside of ladies such as my mom, la Sra. Maria Quintanilla, la Sra. Rios (which we lovingly called "Rivers"), and la Sra. Bruna Guzman. My favorite, however, was the time working in the cotton fields with my sister-in-law Julia on my brother's land south of Tulia on the Caraway and Hutto farms. My sister-in-law taught me many songs and we loved to sing and harmonize in the fields. The days were long and hot but it sure helped to pass the time with our singing. The majority of our extended families moved to other parts of the country where they settled and raised their families. Nevertheless, seasonal crop work was done by our parents and relatives. We learned at a very early age all about harvest, planting, cleaning, and everything pertaining to agriculture.

Many years later, I have come to see this agricultural work done by Mexican nationals and people from many other central and south American countries. American citizens do not want to continue to do this type of manual, seasonal, and back breaking work. Our older siblings and cousins didn't start school till

October and only attending until April when all the migrant population began to move in search of work. After school activities such as summer baseball, summer camp, and swimming were not in our lives. Occasionally we went to the lakes around the Sherman, Whitewright, and Dennison areas. Migrant children played baseball and kickball in the streets and empty lots of neighborhoods. Many skills were developed there. Even as a youngster and all the way through the summer of my senior year in high school, I worked chopping cotton and worked in the sugar beet fields with my cousins in Hart, Texas.

When cotton picking time came (as there were no cotton stripping machines at the time) I loved to go to the cotton fields with my Uncle Pedro who took crews out to the fields. Youngsters as well as adults worked in these fields for long hours every day. Many people picked cotton dragging their cotton sacks behind them and having them weighed by an old-fashioned scale. My job was to keep up with how many pounds of cotton were picked by each individual per day and entering them in a log book my uncle taught me how to use. Cotton pickers were paid by the pounds of cotton they had picked by the end of the week. I was amazed at how many people could pick over eight hundred pounds a day.

The highlight of my summer was when Swisher County celebrated its birthday and the carnival was coming to town! The Ferris wheel, the Hammer, and the tilt-a-whirl were my favorite rides. There was such excitement in the air. I loved this week with its games, rides, food booths, parade, the community barbeque, and sidewalk sales, especially the ones at Huxford's, City Drug, and of course the penny-one cent sale at Bates-Mahaney shoe store. Such bargains! We rarely went out of town to shop. We supported our local grocery stores such as Food Town, Bill's Market, White Auto Store, Caroline's Grocery, Perry's, Huxford's, J-Gee's, and other businesses in town.

Again, I saw no Hispanics or Blacks working in any of these businesses. School was put on the back burner as it took as many workhands as possible to support families. To these working families, there was no such thing as government assistance and food stamps. Family life as we knew it back in the early '50s was quite different than in this day and age. All children chipped in to make sure the whole family was fed, clothed, and had shelter. If illnesses or death came, then we all chipped in to help the grieving families. There was no such thing as WIC, GoFundMe, or other aid for families with dependent children. Our parents had come from descendants that had survived the world war where rationing of food and gas was commonplace. My dad kept old coupons back from when there was rationing of sugar, flour, and even gas. These coupons were not government assistance. They were coupons to keep up with how much of these provisions you had already purchased. During the coronavirus pandemic, we have experienced much of the same with stores limiting the amounts of things one could purchase at one time. "Shelter in Place" and "social distancing" have become the norm. I can understand why it is important to keep a safe distance from one another at a time when not only the United States is in crisis, but every country in the world. My beloved Italy has been hit hard with this virus. I have such wonderful memories of all my trips to Italy. I was totally disappointed in the group of teenagers in the news in Florida that went on with their spring break activities. One young man was even caught on camera as saying, "If I get the coronavirus, I get the coronavirus. At the end of the day, it is not going to keep me from partying." I felt a sense of anger and "sentimiento" at his comments which I felt had so little regard for human life. He later apologized publicly for his off-the-cuff and heartless remarks.

My siblings and I had no free or reduced lunches in the school cafeterias. We all carried our lunches to school and walked to school. I remember young junior high school Black and Hispanic children working in the cafeteria cleaning tables, emptying trash cans, sweeping, and mopping the floors to pay for their lunches and the lunches of their younger siblings. I rarely saw any Anglo children doing this work. There was no shame on the part of my siblings to do this work. We had been taught that we must work for anything we got and school lunches were no exception. Mexican and Black children had to eat upstairs in an old balcony of the Dallas Street Gym. Once again, division was quite evident. After lunch, the youngest Mexican and Black children and the Anglo junior high students went out for after lunch recess, while our older brothers and sisters worked in the cafeteria. I remember Mrs. Crocker, who was the cafeteria manager making arrangements with my parents to allow my siblings to work in the cafeteria. Milk was two cents and came in a little glass bottle and we all thought we were stepping in high cotton when we got to purchase an extra bottle of milk with our own money. There was a snack store across the street from the junior high school, run by a lady named Mrs. Mildred. Most children were forbidden to go there, but most children found themselves there at one time or another. It was a big deal to go to the "Hornet's Nest" as the little store was called. There were many a scuffle or fight behind the "Hornet's Nest" on a regular basis. The high school kids would frequently come down to get a hamburger and coke. Anglo kids were forbidden by their parents to go there, but they disobeyed their parents and found their way there as well. My siblings and I never got to eat there because they were working in the cafeteria to pay for our lunches. After school, the Hornet's Nest was open selling candy, cinnamon toothpicks, pickles, and other things youngsters liked. Candy cigarettes were popular so many kids bought them and pretended to smoke. I remember on one occasion asking my dad if I could try a cigarette. I had never seen my parents smoke, but I had seen one of my brothers smoke "a las escondidas" (hidden). My dad said that it was a nasty, expensive, and time-consuming activity. I insisted that some of the people who smoked looked "cool". He went downtown and bought me a pack of cigarettes and instructed me to smoke. He knew what he was doing. I didn't. I almost choked on the first one, but I continued.

I wanted to find out on my own what was so grand about smoking. I continued to smoke till I made myself sick. After a while, I told my dad that I was finished as I felt sick to my stomach. "Santo remedio" (remedy), I have never touched a cigarette since. My dad never mentioned it to me again and I did likewise. Again, separated from the white children. Our parents did not provide rides to school no matter how cold it was or how many blocks from school we lived. That was pretty common back in the fifties. Unless it was pouring rain or a blizzard, children were expected to walk to school, unless they lived in the country in which case they would take the school bus. For the older children in school, extra-curricular activities and sports were out of the question. They were not allowed to be on school teams because children only attended school certain seasons. I noticed during this time in my life that bullying was pretty commonplace. I remember walking with my siblings and neighbors and kids would throw rocks and dirt as be passed by their well-manicured lawns. We were always careful not to step on any yards because our parents would be very angry and disappointed in us.

My parents had distinct methods of discipline. My mother would swat us with a fly swatter, chunk a house shoe, a "chancla", at us, and threatened to tell my dad when he got home from work as to our unacceptable behavior. My dad was the main disciplinarian. He would talk to us (lecture us) for forty-five minutes about what we had done wrong and to come up with a suitable solution to mend our ways. There was no such thing as "time out" or "get in the corner". Many times, I would just as soon he take the belt and whip us and get it over with, but no! First the offense, then the lecture, then the solution to the problem and the form of punishment to keep us from making the same mistakes. We learned very early in life to not do things that would cause us to have to apologize. My oldest brother, on the other hand, took to heart the saying "es mejor pedir perdon que pedir permiso" (It is better to apologize that to ask permission when the bad deed was already done).

My mother told us "cuentos" at night. My favorite was of these legends were "La Llorona" and "Dancing with a Ghost" which were considered supernatural tales. She told us that her mother and older sisters loved to tell these tales to their children and younger siblings. They were passed on by word of mouth. My grandmother Antonia liked to tell us humorous tales such as "La Hormiga y El Raton" (The Ant and the Mouse) and "La Pan-adera" (The Baker). All these tales had a hidden message which was intended to teach us lessons in life. We didn't know it at the time, we just enjoyed being entertained with tales from yester-year. My uncle Joe (Chema) was always making up tales to scare us. He managed to get his message across, but was all in good fun. It wasn't until much later that I read some of these tales translated to English. At about that time I began to see cliques forming, groups of the same ethnic backgrounds forming these groups. I never considered them to be gangs as we know them today, but the Mexican kids formed groups usually of junior high or high school age children. Some called themselves "Pachucos".

They wanted to resemble the gangs of larger cities but in Tulia it was almost impossible and with the discipline of our parents, it was made doubly hard. My older brother was part of a group. They weren't the Pachucos but they were like the watch dogs. They didn't break the law but they went after those that intimidated young kids or innocent adults. Some of these groups liked to wear khakis and white t-shirts. They were known for protecting the younger Hispanic children from being victims of rock throwing and name calling. My younger brother was not a part of any of those groups. He and his friends hung out at each other's houses and played street basketball or baseball in empty lots. Blacks and whites also had small groups who hung out together. For years, I had seen Blacks and Mexicans hang out together. There were not many Black families living in Knox County when my family lived there.

Upon our arrival in Swisher County in 1956, there were very few Black and Hispanic families. All the way through elementary, junior high, and high school, there were very few Black students enrolled. About eight to ten percent of the student population was Hispanic my entire school career at Tulia schools. I never saw much physical activity among any of the groups, but verbal attacks were quite common. Since we never heard our parents cuss, it was quite foreign to us. To this day, my sister spells out "H-E-double-L" instead of just uttering the word "Hell". That's just the way we were taught. "Maldiciones" (curse words) were forbidden in our home. However, I did feel a sense of security as we walked to school to have all the big kids defend us little kids from the rock throwing and name-calling we suffered.

I often wondered about the children in big dangerous cities, if they went through the same things. I once asked my cousins who were raised in East LA if they went through this. They told me that most gangs left them alone because they never paid much mind to their activities. Kids who talked back to gang members were often recruited to join them or attack them. I always felt like this was so unnecessary and ridiculous. Our California cousins could tell us scary stories about gangs. Living in East Los Angeles, our cousin's parents worked quite a distance from their jobs. My aunt told us about having to take two or three different city busses to get to her job. She said she would leave around 5 a.m. to get to her 7 a.m. job. The children would have to make their way to school. They were lucky that their paternal grandparents lived next door to them. Their grandmother would have a snack ready for them when they returned from school. Even though they lived in the city of Los Angeles, they lived through many acts of racism and prejudice. Their upbringing was quite different from our upbringing. They experienced much the same of what we did being raised in a small Texas town. Why did different ethnic groups fight against each other? What was gained? What did one group gain by belittling and hurting another group? Where did we get this from? Again, a learned behavior. Trying to fit in, even if in a negative way was desired by some. Children are not born prejudiced, judgmental, or being a racist. They see it somewhere. Children do learn to do what they see.

My siblings got their exercise by carrying water, chopping wood for the wooden stoves, and keeping the house and the yard tidy and clean. My dad and my brothers got jobs at the compress, my brothers during the day and my father at night. Behind the compress warehouses were barracks where some of the compress workers lived in small rooms. I remember entire families lived there. The cost to rent those barracks was minimal. Again, only Hispanic and Black families lived there, no Anglos. I am not implying that all Anglos were well off. There were some Anglo families that were dirt poor as well and they too were discriminated against even by other Anglos. In Tulia, there were two labor camps called "el campito" where several families lived in one or two rooms of the building. One was across from Taylor-Evans farm store the other was east of town on the Silverton highway. In this day and age, I still see this division in Swisher County. Many of the Anglo families were hard working families as well but better jobs were afforded them by the store merchants and other business owners. I remember that as a child, we lived on South Donley. The south side was where all the Mexican-American people lived. It was called "el barrio", which literally just means "the neighborhood". The Black families lived in the northwest part of town across the railroad tracks in a section called "sunset addition". That section of town was also call "the flats". I always wondered and asked why we all lived divided. I was always curious as to why certain people lived in a certain part of town. Even the churches were designated for whites, Blacks, and Mexicans. The Blacks had and still have a church in "sunset addition". Downtown, close to the bus station, I would see a sign that would say "No Blacks Allowed". This early part of my childhood, I spent my days playing with the other neighborhood children who were not old enough to attend school. There were no kindergarten classes at that time. When children started school, they started in the first grade. I was always curious about reading and learning as my three other siblings had books and homework. I was jealous. My parents always bought us the Golden Books to read. My sister would be reading about the *Adventures of Dick and Jane*. I wanted so much to read about Spot, their dog, and about Sally, the little sister. My dad taught us to read in English and Spanish when we were very young. He used the Sunday school books designed for children and the ones designed for adults and I would read them from cover to cover never being satisfied because I craved that need to read. That is when my dad started letting me find certain scriptures in the Bible to read and study. I played a game with my dad which we called "Memorize a Bible Verse". My dad would give me a nickel or a privilege every time I memorized a Bible verse and could quote it verbatim. The object was to see if I could quote it and tell the name of the book and chapter and verse. My very first one to memorize was John 3:16 – "for God so loved the world that He gave his only begotten Son so that whoever believeth in Him should not perish but have everlasting life." I got an extra nickel or privilege if I could recite the verse in Spanish. I was so proud when I quoted to him, "Por que de tal manera amo Dios al mundo que ha dado a su hijo unigenito, para que todo aquel que en el cree no se pierda mas tenga vida eterna." That day, I earned a dime or got to play an extra half hour with my cousins or just riding my bike. My mother was instrumental in helping me learn my verses. I remember once that I had put learning a verse on the back burner and I ran to my mom in search of a verse to memorize. She came to my rescue by having me recite John 11:35, "Jesus wept" in English and "Jesus lloró" in Spanish! Go mom! I earned another dime or time to play hopscotch! She, however, didn't let me off the hook. She told me the story of Lazarus and what had caused Jesus to weep. I absolutely loved reading the Bible, especially the parables. They were fascinating and my dad made them come alive with their explanation and how they applied to people like us. He taught a Sunday School class for adults for close to thirty years. That is where I got my love of scripture. Sunday was reserved for rest and church. Sundays also brought special meals such as fried chicken or pot roast. I never remember not going to church. My parents were made sure we were there every Sunday morning and evening. We enjoyed a great spiritual upbringing. Nothing brings more joy to a child as to see their parents worship. My mother had been brought up in the Roman Catholic church (where we got a love for traditions) and my father had been raised Protestant by the elderly couple who raised him after the death of his parents. This elderly couple was church-going and instilled in my dad the need to have God in his life. As a child, I learned a lot of life's lessons and traditions by word of mouth. Parents used stories to teach us to handle life events and the struggles to overcome trials. That is why I am convinced that people of yesteryear learned not only by written scripture but also by word-of-mouth stories and practices which became traditional, thus tradition along with the written word caused our religiosity to evolve into what we have today. I learned later on in my religious studies how Jesus used parables in much the same way. When asked by his followers why he spoke in parables, he responded, "so the people would understand."

I was so influenced by my dad's love of scripture that later in life (much later) I was enrolled in Biblical studies offered by the diocese of Amarillo and proudly earned my certification in Advanced Biblical Studies. My oldest sister was also influenced by him as she graduated from LABI in Ysleta, Texas also earning her Biblical Studies certification. As soon as I was old enough to go to school, I was more than ready and very eager to join the ranks of the neighborhood kids who walked the sixteen blocks to East Ward.

What an adventure! A whole group of neighborhood kids walked together through town passing Piggly Wiggly, The Royal Theatre, Simpson's Motor Sales, and Tulia Steam Laundry. Arriving early at school, we gathered with everyone waiting for the school bell which would signal us to enter the doors. We were so proud to have our school boxes with the supplies that we would be using in the classroom. I remember entering my first grade room for the first time and seeing that everyone in that room was Mexican. I had mixed feelings about that. On one hand, I knew almost everyone there but on the other hand, the nagging question always stuck in the back of my young mind as to why we were separated from the Anglos. Again, separation, in our neighborhood, in our churches, and now in our schools. No one seemed to want to address my questions. My parents simply told us to go to school, be courteous and polite, follow the rules, learn as much as possible, and not to create any problems for the teacher. They taught us that our teachers were there to teach us and not to disrespect them in any form or fashion. In other words, in my home, the teacher was next to God. We looked at our teachers with eyes of fascination. I remember thinking, I would like to be a teacher someday, but I had no idea if it was possible since I didn't see any Hispanic teachers in the entire school system.

I got my first chance to be a teacher as a first grader. My first grade teacher didn't know one word of Spanish and many of my first grade classmates didn't know a word of English. Bingo! I knew both languages well. I could speak both! In fact, I could read and write in both languages! Thanks to my parents who had the presence of mind to not only instill the love of learning but the love of sharing that knowledge. I got my first teaching opportunity one Wednesday morning when recess time came and everyone was so excited to go to the playground. I worked up the nerve to ask my teacher if I could read to the kids in small groups. Low and behold she said yes and I was over the moon with excitement!

When we went back inside, she gave me a group of five children to read to. She took a group of five children to form a reading group and gave the others some math fact sheets to work on while we read with our little group. I read to the kids, my classmates in English, translating to Spanish the words and parts of the story they didn't understand. It was great fun! This went on for a few months when I realized that we were not using the same books as the children in the other first grade rooms. Seems like all we did was read a little, do a little arithmetic, and color a lot. I loved to color but enough was enough! Learning the math facts was not terribly exciting since I played school with my sister and the neighborhood kids and we had gotten math flashcards from my parents for Christmas and frankly, they were beginning to be boring. I read every book I could get my hands on and for my Spanish reading, it was nearly always the Bible, as very few books were published in Spanish for children. I must interject here, that I was such a sponge for learning that I sat nightly by my dad's side as he prepared meaningful lessons for his adult Sunday school class. He studied in Spanish and English and I marveled as his having such command of both languages. I not only marveled at his command of both languages but of his being ambidextrous! I've tried this many times, but fail miserably every time. My siblings and I grew up to become true bilinguals. My mom insisted that we speak Spanish well and my dad insisted that we speak English well as it was the language of instruction in the public schools. I felt very fortunate to be able to have good command of both languages. I felt such a sense of pride being bilingual and bicultural. All my cousins were bilingual as well… that pride became short lived when we entered the public school. Things began to change. Our teachers would forbid us to speak Spanish at school. We were punished for using a language "foreign" to them. At six years of age, I was at a loss as to why speaking Spanish was so wrong! Why couldn't we communicate in two languages? Why didn't they know Spanish? How come they knew only English? Was there something wrong with knowing two languages? Was English superior to Spanish? Why could they only communicate in only one language, after all they were educators! I had all these questions on my mind and all my parents would discuss with me was that I was to obey my teachers and not to question them. They were in charge and I was to follow their rules and instruction. As inquisitive and outspoken as I was, I wanted to know why, why, why? Spanish was the language of my grandparents, my parents, my aunts and uncles, my cousins, my church! Why was it forbidden? I didn't see this as oppression perhaps because I was too young to know what oppression was! I was obedient to my parents and did my best to keep my six-year-old opinions to myself. At that young age, I had no clue why people with dark skins were looked at different than people with fair skin. Even my siblings, who were all lighter skinned than I was, dared to give me a bath with a little bleach and scrub me with a Brillo-pad to see if they could lighten my skin. They wanted my skin to be lighter and maybe then I would be more easily accepted by my classmates! Imagine that! My parents had quite a bit to say about that when they returned home! Why was it forbidden to the point of being punished for speaking our dominant language? Sometimes I would hear my teachers telling Spanish speaking students that it was wrong to speak a language the not everyone understood because others might get the impression that you were talking about them. In my six-year-old mind I would think, I wouldn't talk about my classmates in a language they didn't understand. I would talk to and about them in a language they did understand so that we could hold conversations, play games, read, and study together. I figured that it would be a complete waste of time talking to them in a language they didn't understand! It was at this young age that I began to see that separation of children by ethnic groups and languages spoken was a learned behavior, taught to children by the adults around them. What did I know about prejudice and racism? It was then that I remember younger parents not teaching their children to be bilingual because there was a certain stigma to speaking a "foreign" language. I began to question what could possibly be wrong with speaking two languages? Why was it so wrong and forbidden in the public school? As a child I tried to teach my young friends to speak Spanish but was abruptly stopped and was told in no uncertain terms that "English" was the official language. The teaching profession was looked at as such an honorable profession that I dreamed of being a teacher someday. Through the years, this noble profession was downgraded to a profession which was not held to as high esteem as in the past. I noticed later on during the Covid-19 pandemic, when parents had to take on the role of home school teacher, that I began to see a better appreciation for the teaching profession. Parents found out that teaching wasn't "a piece of cake" as some would have said it in the past. I saw the old adage, "those who can't, teach" abruptly change during the pandemic to, "those who CAN, teach". What lessons we learn by living and going through trials of other professions. People are now beginning to understand that teaching is not "glorified baby-sitting". There is a hard lesson to learn in judging a profession one knows little of.

I have always held the medical profession in high esteem. Both my sisters became nurses as did a number of my nieces. Anyone in the medical profession is a hero in my eyes. To tend to the sick is a calling from above and I admire those who will answer the call to care for those sick and dying. I spent forty-two years of my life in the field of education, so I can't even pretend to know what health professionals go through. I just know that I am very appreciative of them knowing that they want to be there, particularly in this time of the coronavirus pandemic. All the first responders are to be commended and appreciated for putting their lives on the line to help those suffering from any illness. The families of first responders are also heroes in my book. All professions have their place in our society. We should not overlook their importance in the circle of life.

People who serve in the military rank up there in importance in my book. Willingly serving to protect the rights of all people is surely a calling. I see so many protesters take for granted the right and privilege of being free to protest and make their opinion known. Peaceful demonstration is a right as well as a privilege, but when rioting to the point of destruction of life and property becomes a part of these protests, I don't support that. So "black lives matter" should be "all lives matter". Everyone counts, even the unborn child. Those lives matter because all life beings are created in the image of God. How quickly we forget that it is God who knew us before we were born, before we took our first breath. Yet part of society thinks it is ok to abort. Everyone's contribution to make this world work is important. No one is more important than anyone else. Regardless of ethnic background, color of skin, level of education, or socioeconomic status, that should not make one group superior to the others. We are all created equal and made in the image of God. I love Psalm 139, which tells us that we, all of us, every person from the womb to the tomb as human beings who bear the image of God. "Fearfully and wonderfully made" means God intimately knows every person and all humanity belongs to him. And in the verses 13-14 which state, "For you formed my inward parts; you knitted me together in my mother's womb. I praise you, for I am fearfully and wonderfully made." We tend to forget this and only pay it lip service when convenient.

I read in one documentary one in four Black American Black men are incarcerated in this "land of the free". There is something wrong with this picture. We have the highest rate of incarcerated individuals of any country in the world. Permanent change needs to come but what is the answer? I don't believe violent protesting is the answer to this problem. Many may feel that peaceful protesting gets nowhere and that we must defund the police. I believe that defunding the police would be a mistake. Would it become a free-for-all if distinct constructive measures were not put in place? We have all heard the adage, violence begets violence, so what are we learning from all this violence? It is not right to unjustly punish or kill the innocent (abortion included), but it is also not right to violently destroy or damage the properties of individuals who have worked tirelessly to build their businesses from the ground up to have them destroyed in the path of violence and marches for justice. Racial profiling is wrong. I once experienced racial profiling in a particular store at South Plains Mall in Lubbock, Texas. My sister and I were looking at purses and gloves in this department store.

We were speaking in Spanish (our primary language) when I heard a clerk tell another clerk, "Watch those Mexicans like a hawk. They look and look at things and never buy anything. If they go to another department, follow them as they tend to shop-lift."

My sister and I went on to buy a few things and when we approached the check out, I paid with a credit card and told the lady that they had very nice things.

She said to me "Oh, you speak English?"

I answered in a most meticulous English voice, "Yes ma'am I do."

She turned every shade of red imaginable. She assumed that just because we were not fair-skinned and spoke Spanish we must not be trusted. I've often told my Anglo friend that when a group of Mexicans are together, they normally tend to speak in their mother tongue. I give them an example – I say, if a group of Anglos were together (even if they spoke another language) they would normally fall back to their mother tongue. This is human nature folks!

During my elementary school years, I was told by my Anglo friends that they could earn a nickel every time they turned someone in for speaking Spanish. I was careful to speak English around those children. At this young age, I could see young children report back or tattle on children speaking Spanish. They, unbeknownst to them, were being set up for pre-judging others. They may not have understood why this was so wrong, but if their teachers told them to behave that way, it must be ok! I thought a nickel was great money since you could buy a lemon or a pickle at the local grocery store. It wasn't until a few years later that I learned that that was not true. English is not the official language of Texas. I learned that English is the official language of trade and of instruction in the public schools. I continued to speak Spanish where and when I could. In our circle of friends and relatives, it was pretty common to speak a mixture of Spanish and English thus using an English word made into a Spanish word by adding a Spanish verb ending and VOILA! Spanglish was born (to me anyway – I didn't know until much later that the term Spanglish is pretty common.) I remember my brothers and sisters using such "Spanglish" words such as "espeliar" – to spell, "feiliar" – to fail, "flunkiar" - to flunk. I now often think of how many English words we use using that same method. Some of my Anglo friends even tried to make English words sound Spanish by adding an "O" to the end of a Spanish word to make it an English word. One of my favorite plays on words was when groups of young (and old) men of the town played baseball. Some of the terms I remember them using were ones such as "batear" - to bat, "estraiquiar" - to strike, "pichar" -to pitch, and "cachar" - to catch! What things we do to slaughter our beautiful languages of English and Spanish! Shifting easily from one language to another is quite common among people who are bilingual.

One can almost make a game of coming up with word changes and "dichos" (sayings, endearments) which not all have literal translations. Endearments such as sweetheart and darling sound ridiculous and make no sense in another language. My parents were so adamant that we speak both languages well so all my siblings and I became totally fluent in both languages as far as reading, writing, and speaking which proved to me later in life to be most useful. My dad loved to read scripture to me as he prepared his lesson for each Sunday. I was intrigued with the teachings of scripture that I challenged myself to quote certain scripture in both languages. It became a game I played by myself at home as I was forbidden to share my language experiences with my friends and classmates. I was stunned to learn that even in religious studies, we were divided. Spanish speakers went to Spanish worship services and English speakers went to English worship services. At our church services, I felt right at home because the singing, the preaching, Sunday school lessons were taught in Spanish. I remember our church was considered a "mission" of the Anglo church of the same denomination. I have fond memories of Mr. Mal Wynne and Mrs. Betty Devin coming over to play the piano and lead the singing. Miss Mattie Devin gave me a red Bible that I treasure to this day. I always had a yearning to worship with my school classmates, but I rarely brought up the subject.

I remember going on a retreat with the Methodist Youth Fellowship (known as the MYF) and sharing scripture with Richard Edwards and Becky Teel. How blessed I felt that finally the Mexican kids could attend these outings at Ceta Glen, a beautiful canyon campsite near Wayside. I often wondered why this division existed. All my Mexican friends in church spoke English, we could function in either language, Spanish or English. Even though the language of the Black community was English, they had their own church with other Blacks. They all spoke English! Go figure! The English language was the first language of Anglos and Blacks, so why the division? I wondered why this was such an issue. If everyone spoke two languages – problem solved, we would go from one language to another without a problem then the divisions would stop. I have since learned that the Spanish speaking churches now have services in English because these younger generations have stopped teaching their children Spanish because of the backlash of speaking Spanish when they were young. It is not uncommon to see Hispanic youngsters not speak a word of Spanish even though their grandparents don't speak fluent English. Where has communication gone? I see Hispanic youngsters of all ages in this day in age that are ashamed to speak Spanish in public, or even at home.

I once heard a young neighbor of mine shout at his mother, "Don't talk to me in Spanish! It's embarrassing!"

My heart went out to that mother as she had spoken to her children English and Spanish all along and now her child was annoyingly addressing his mother with such disrespect! I believe that disrespect goes hand in hand with racism and prejudice. At what point did this young man become so adamant and demanding with his mother? This all stemmed from the fact that their grandparents were ridiculed and punished for speaking Spanish. I see children not speaking the language of their grandparents and I am deeply saddened by this.

I remember when I turned seven in November and in December, my dad introduced me to a very nice man, a friend of his by the name of H.M. Baggerly. He was a newspaper editor and had his newspaper business in the same building as the old radio station KTUE (1260) on your radio dial. That always stuck with me! Mr. Baggerly published a newspaper weekly, the *Tulia Herald*, "Covering Swisher County like the Sunshine". I loved that title. As a child, I thought that was such a cool name. Sunshine was such a marvelous wonder because as a child, I loved to be outside in the sunshine as most other children did as well. I feel like children in this day and age don't love the sunshine like we did – phones, tablets, iPads, and television have taken over and consume so much of children's lives today. I also marveled at the radio station and the ability to talk on the radio. I remember Mr. Baggerly asking me to sing Christmas carols on the radio in both languages! I was thrilled to be able to sing "Silent Night" and "Noche de Paz". I was so proud that I had memorized two verses in both languages. Mr. Baggerly always encouraged me to stay with both languages and for the first time I was so proud that a non-Spanish speaker actually thought this was a good thing. Then I would enter a store and be reminded that I was to use English only. I remember that on the west side of the square stood a phone booth and a water fountain with a sign above them that said, "Whites only". I couldn't understand why. A local business even had a sign that read, "No Negros Allowed". Again, I felt the sting of prejudice among the townspeople. People have a way of hurting other human beings by being non-inclusive of other cultures and of other ethnic backgrounds. We even had two barbershops in town, one for the whites and one for the Mexicans. I did on occasion see some Anglos getting their hair cut at Luera's Barber Shop on South Austin.

As my first grade year was coming to an end at East Ward, I knew that we would all be spending another year in first grade for failure to master the English language. I begged my dad to go to the school and speak to Mr. Mitchell who was the principal at the time. I wanted him to know that I needed to go on. I needed to move on to the next grade. I could do the work! I was certain of it. Mr. Mitchell listened and I was promptly moved to Mrs. Wynne's first grade room where I was to spend the last six weeks of my first grade year to prove that I was ready to move on to second grade. Talk about jumping for joy! My father was instrumental in having other parents question why their child was not in a regular first grade room. As a result, a few other Hispanic children in my first grade room were moved to a regular first grade room and managed to pass to the second grade. I went in wholeheartedly immersing myself in everything I could and voila! I passed to the second grade! I was in heaven! I hated to leave my Spanish speaking classmates but I was ready for this new adventure! That summer I spent day after day perfecting my grammar skills, reading the *Highlights* magazines I had received for Christmas and begging my parents to buy me those learning books they sold at Perry's and Ben Franklin's because I was determined never to stay behind. My parents bought me flashcards so I could learn math facts. My dad tried to teach me figuring percentages in my head as he did but to no avail, I didn't inherit math skills as my older brothers did. Reading has always been where my strength is. I began to notice how Hispanics or Blacks were not asked for their opinions about things concerning our community and in our school system. I began to see how discrimination grew and grew among the different ethnic groups in our community.

Working at night, my dad rarely attended public meetings in our community and school. I saw that all business owners, merchants, doctors, nurses, and teachers were all Anglo. All service jobs were held by Hispanics and Blacks. All farms were owned by Anglos, most of whom had inherited the family farms from their parents and grandparents, but I noticed that the hired hands in agriculture were Hispanic or Black. The custodial jobs and housekeeping jobs were held by Hispanics and Blacks. My dad even secured a job as a maintenance worker at the school. There was stigma attached to that type of work which still exists today.

I questioned many things in my young life. My parents tried to satisfy my curiosity by buying me books to read. My dad even got us a few encyclopedia books that had been discarded so that I could satisfy my need to read. Even an old torn Webster's dictionary was one of my prized possessions. Missing more than a few pages was ok with me. To this day, I have that old dictionary, a Spanish-English dictionary and a French-English dictionary, that saved my life while study the three languages. I later acquired a New Testament in English and French side by side. I still can't bring myself to google everything to find the answers. Yes, I still use the dictionary. I'm old school.

Enter the first day of my second grade year at East Ward, My new teacher – Mrs. Billie Love. I absolutely loved her. She was beautiful and glamorous in the eyes of any second grader. She wore high heels that clicked as she walked down the hall. She was fun and interested in everyone's learning. She sat us in groups of four desks. She didn't separate us from the Anglos or the Blacks. This was awesome. I got to sit with a different group every six weeks so that we would get to know everyone in our self-contained second grade room. Mr. Wynne was the music teacher. He wanted the choir robes to be made by the parents and of course I volunteered my mother as she was an excellent seamstress. My mother made choir robes along with the other mothers. I didn't get to sing with the choir in that Christmas program because I had the flu. I cried for days, but finally got over it. Each room had a room mother who was in charge of getting the other mothers to help plan the parties for the year. I so clearly remember Mrs. Marie Brietling being the room mother for Mrs. Love's room. She was to ask a group of mothers to help her in the planning of the parties. Once again, I volunteered my mother to Mrs. Brietling and I was thrilled when she called my mother and asked her to be in the committee. What an honor it was for me for my mother to be a part of my room's activity planning. I was so happy that she was included even though I had volunteered her, she graciously accepted and was a part of all my activities that year. This was the highlight of my second grade year. Everything was an adventure. My grades were good as I could do all my classwork with no problem. I was no longer worried that I was looked down on or turned in for speaking Spanish. I learned to not go against the grain and only speak English around those who felt threatened by my speaking Spanish. I learned to adjust to any uncomfortable situation. Even at this young age, I was learning that prejudice was a learned behavior. Young Anglo children in their innocence wanted to play with us but were forbidden to by their parents. Those young children didn't know why but they obeyed their parents and some of them soon began to demonstrate a degree of prejudice and discrimination among children their own age. I was almost sorry to see the end of my second grade year come to an end but I knew summer was coming and I would enjoy every single day of the carefree days of playing in the sun and in the street (yes, we played in the street), drank water from the water hose, and were delighted when a fire hydrant spewed out water in which we readily played. Fun times were ahead to be able to play with my neighbors, playing such games as hopscotch, "Mother, may I?", and red light, green light!

In the summer, my brothers went to work in the fields. Two of my aunts and uncles and cousins lived within walking distance of my house. I had an uncle and his family that lived in Hart, TX and an aunt and family that lived in Olton, TX so we had family close enough to Tulia so we could visit often. My mother was so family oriented that she insisted that my dad take us to Munday, TX at least one weekend a month to visit my grandparents. That was wonderful as many cousins gathered at my grandparents' house on certain weekends and holidays. Besides my mother, she had twelve siblings who loved and still love to gather to celebrate holidays. My grandparents lived on a small five-acre farm in Knox County. They had an old barn and an area where they kept feed for the pigs and chickens. They had two peach trees and an old well in the backyard. All the cousins had a great time at that farm. We would take long walks into town as the farm was only a few miles from the city limit. There was a cellar in the backyard beside the well. What fun it was to get water from the well for the pigs, throw food in their sty, and watch them scramble for the corn we gave them. Our Uncle Joe lived with my grandparents, so we were close to him as well. He loved to make tamales and empanadas with his sisters (my aunts) that came to visit. I had such a special relationship with my grandfather Leon Perez. He was awesome. He loved telling me about the old days. I enjoyed listening to him talk about how they used to travel by covered wagon to their destination where they would do seasonal work. He talked to me about the campfire time he enjoyed with his family as they traveled. I hung on his every word and of course, I was full of questions for him and the old customs and traditions. He told me about his folks and two of his nieces that were very close to him. Years later (by chance) I met one of their sons. We did not know we were related, distantly but nevertheless related. I loved to listen to his stories about family life and the adventures he had during his childhood and teenage years. I would tease him about being so much older than my grandmother. He wasn't that much older, but I loved to tease him about it. I loved to help him polish the brown and white Chevrolet car he kept in the old garage and wash the old pick-up he used at the farm. I would always bring him tons of chocolate candy whenever we went to the farm.

Much to my grandmother's objections, my grandfather and I devoured the chocolate candy. Easter was my favorite time to go to my grandparents' house because of the Easter egg hunts and "los cascarones", confetti eggs. The chasing around and breaking the confetti-filled eggshells on my cousin's heads was great fun. Even cracking a confetti egg on my grandfather's head was acceptable. Breaking one on my grandmother's head was totally out of the question. Young children and teenagers and the young-at-heart joined in the fun. Going to church at Easter was sheer joy! We sang songs about the love shown to us by our Lord and Savior. We learned about death and resurrection, new life, and the joy we shared was contagious. Those songs remain in my head and heart to this day. We would get all dressed up with frilly dresses and frilly socks. My mother could not get a pretty hat on my head. No way was I having that! Church picnics at Easter with our church families was great fun.

The green fields where we had the Easter egg hunts were awesome.

3 My grandmother Antonia was the disciplinarian of the family. She chased us around and forbade us to bother the pigs and to stay away from the peach trees if the peaches were still green. She would warn us not to eat them because we would get sick! Did we listen? Not always! Did we get sick? Always! When the peaches were ripe for the picking, my grandmother and aunts would make pies and little fried pies! We were blessed to be able to see our grandparents every month. My grandparents were bilingual but spoke Spanish with the family when we gathered at their house. My uncle Joe didn't like to speak English so we rarely heard him speak English. When the new school year began, I was so excited to start the third grade! My teacher that year was Mrs. Cora Belle Roberts! How I loved that lady! She loved role playing and always had little productions that we participated in. That year was so special because in the Easter play. I got the part of the Easter Bunny. No separation of church and state here. She believed in me! I learned all my parts

without a hitch. She let me use my imagination and allowed me to be creative. However, all wasn't smooth sailing the rest of my elementary school years. We continued to be discriminated against. There were those teachers who still couldn't trust us to do well in extra-curricular activities. We still didn't get the opportunities to run for student council or try out for speaking parts in plays and later on in cheerleading. Some went as far as to tell us that they knew we couldn't afford it. It became customary for us to hang out with only our cousins and other Mexican-American children because Anglos didn't allow us to go into their houses. I never could understand why.

When I was in the fourth grade, we moved to North Austin Street. We were the only Hispanic family on that street. A year or so after that, another Hispanic family moved a few doors down from us. Even our Hispanic friends wondered why we had left the "barrio". We would often be told by our Anglo friends that their parents didn't want us to come to their house because Hispanics shouldn't be living in this white neighborhood. I often wondered what a white folk's house looked like on the inside. Were they that much different than us? What was the difference? Our Anglo friends obeyed their parents and didn't let us in their houses. My mom told me to invite my friends over. I did. My Anglo friend told me that she would not be telling her mother about going in my house because she (in her words), "Would have hell to pay". After coming in my house, she found out that my house was no different than hers. In fact, she made the comment,

"All your beds are made!" Can you imagine? Why? Weren't everybody's beds made? After all it was after school! We played Barbies and we played Old Maid cards with my sister. We played a game called "Pollyanna" – how I loved that game which is similar to "Sorry". I have looked for that game with no luck – even Amazon let me down! My Anglo friend was surprised and said, "You all do the same things we do!" Did she think because we were Mexican we would be so different? One of my Anglo friends even made the comment that we ate the same kinds of foods that they did. They had always had the impression that all we ate was tacos, enchiladas, tortillas, and beans! That was the beginning of when I began to think that prejudice and racism is a learned behavior. Children learn what they are taught from their first teachers – their parents! Of course, at that time in my life I was naïve. I thought all people were taught the same lessons. I had a lot to learn.

Living in the "white" part of town was an eye-opener for me. There was a family next door that did allow their children to play with us – the Devol family. Those children had been taught as we had been to respect other people and their property. My new found friend went to our elderly neighbor's house to help them clean up their yard and help them throw out their trash. This was so rewarding to us and our parents always encouraged us to help our elderly neighbors. Some of them were old school however and were leery of letting a little Mexican in their yard. They eventually came around and let us pick flowers form their gardens for our mother. Living on North Austin was quite an experience for me. I missed all my Hispanic friends but I was learning to adjust and make the most of my new neighborhood and continued to make friends. One of my aunts and her family moved to Bowie Street and I was happy! I had a cousin my age a block and a half and I was thrilled. Some of my other cousins moved to south Dallas Street and that was just about ten blocks from my house. My aunts and my mother were sisters and so life was good. We played volleyball till all hours of the night using the clothesline or rope tied between to trees as a net. That's when I learned that necessity is the mother of invention. We had to make do because we didn't have the money to spare to buy an honest to goodness volleyball set. As a young child, I always felt the need to be surrounded by family. We spent hours playing with our cousins, forming a bond that exists to this day. My mother comes from a family of thirteen, so I have so many relatives that it is impossible to count them all. I have made it a lifetime goal to get to know all my family and I have made a lot of progress. I was fortunate to know all my aunts and uncles and their spouses. I have met countless cousins. In the mid-nineties we began the tradition of holding bi-annual family reunions. These family reunions have been an absolute joy to have! My extended family is enormous and I am happy to be a part of this family.

On the other hand, my dad was an only child, born in Hamlin, Jones County, Texas. Both his parents were only children as well. This was very unusual in a Hispanic family. My paternal grandparents died when my dad was a child. I have absolutely no cousins, aunts, or uncles from this union. I never met my paternal grandparents and the only memories my dad had of them were very vague. I do know that they are both buried in Altus, Oklahoma as my paternal grandmother was Indian from one of the tribes that settled in Oklahoman territory. I feel an emptiness of not knowing this side of my family, but I am thankful that my dad came to be as a result of this union. I learned and inherited so many good things from my dad. The main things being love of God, family, a tremendous work ethic and the love of learning. I also learned from him that we are all created equal and that we should celebrate our uniqueness. My dad never met a stranger. I was always amazed at how my dad would pick up hitchhikers on the road. He would always tell us that he had hitchhiked many a time. He always said that he felt bad for the individuals having to walk and their reasons for having to do so. He said we didn't know their story and what hardship they could be going through. We never questioned his decision to do so. He could carry on a conversation with any man, woman, or child. I think my dad was color-blind as I never heard him say anything about how the color of a person's skin made him/her less of a human being. All were the handiwork of God.

My dad was born in Jones County, Texas in a little town called Hamlin. My mother was also born in Jones County, Texas. They were both children of migrant parents. Their families were acquainted in Jones County. My dad was an orphan at a very young age and was an only child. After his parent's death, he was left all alone, being that my grandfather Lorenzo Delgado and his mother Juanita Olague Delgado were only children as well. My dad didn't have any extended family. My dad was raised by an elderly couple in Knox County. They instilled in him the hunger for learning. However, they both died when my father was a sophomore in high school and from that point on, my dad had to fend for himself. At the age of twenty, my mother and father were married at St. Joseph's Catholic Church in Rhineland, Texas. So even at that young age, my dad was practicing commitment to marriage, love of family, and love of God. Now my mother's family was his new family. How overwhelmed he was to have inherited such a large family. He made it a point to get to know every one of his new brothers-in-law and sisters-in-law and all their children. Maybe that's where I get my desire to know all my relatives. He had an excellent relationship with all of them. I never heard him say an unkind word about any of them. My maternal grandparents loved him and overwhelmed him with fatherly and motherly love to make up for his lack of not having parents any longer.

My mother was the complete opposite of my dad. She was a shy soft-spoken person whom my grandparents called upon for a gentle solution to sibling problems. There were three older sisters and the rest were younger than her. She was a seamstress, loved embroidery, crocheting, and canning. She liked, not loved, to cook. Her specialty was fried chicken and butter rolls. She was not outspoken, so the opposite of my dad. She quietly and gently gave her opinions. She mothered her younger siblings and my very youngest uncle, her baby brother who was fifteen years younger than her was her best friend till her early death at the age of forty-six. He (Tio Marcelino) was thirty-two and was devastated that the sister who cradled him and spoiled him was gone. She had seen him through the birth of five children and loved them as much as she loved him. These five children plus a few more still have a strong relationship with my siblings and me. I was always so proud that I was born on my parent's fifteenth wedding anniversary. I have their marriage certificate and I am very proud of it.

4 At the beginning of my freshman year in high school, my mother passed away when I was fourteen. Two months after my mom passed away, I turned fifteen. She had suffered a stroke five years before when I was nine years old. She had been at the bedside of my sister and sisters-in-law when they had their children. She stayed with them and cared for their families and the newborn babies. After a few (six) weeks, she returned to us. What a celebration that was! She had to be in a wheelchair because her left side was paralyzed. She was determined to walk again and she did. Her physical therapy was done by my sixteen-year-old sister Josie and me. We worked with her, crawled with her, exercised with her, prayed with her, until one day she left that wheel chair and walked only with the use of a cane. A year later, she got rid of the cane and walked on her own without limitation and no cane. She got to be at the birth of other grandchildren and was very grateful for that blessing.

I started my freshman year at Tulia High School without my mother. My sister left to Oklahoma to the job corps in Guthrie. Upon her return, she went to nursing school in Amarillo and was employed as a nurse till her retirement. Her love of geriatrics led her to work in nursing homes. Later, she went to work as an immunization nurse till her retirement. To me, that was certainly a calling. Now both my sisters Isabel and Josie were nurses. How I admired their dedication to their professions. My dad encouraged me to follow in their footsteps and go into nursing but I knew that I could never be a nurse. That was a profession I don't think I could handle. I always teased my sisters when they asked if I would be interested in nursing.

I would always say, "No, I am too afraid that someone would die on my watch and it would be my fault because of my lack of no knowing what to do."

They would always make light of it and say, "Well, that's why you go to nursing school, to learn what to do."

During these years in high school, once again I was reprimanded for speaking Spanish. Once again, I felt that nagging sting as to why I was not allowed to speak my first language. Why was it so wrong? Once again, I was reminded that people around me that didn't speak Spanish would feel as though we were talking about them. This time in my semi-rebellious teenage years I thought to myself maybe that wouldn't be such a bad idea. When my other Spanish speaking friends suggested that we do this, my dad's little voice nagged at my conscience that it would be wrong.

I backed off but came up with a defense mechanism that would pull me through and I would tell those who accused us of talking about them, "If I wanted to talk about you, I would say it in a language that you would understand, so that you would know that you were the subject of our discussion." More than once my dad had to go to Tulia High School to defend my right to speak Spanish. Most bilinguals surf from one language to another without even noticing it. Both languages come so naturally to a true bilingual that it is done without giving it a second thought. Most monolingual persons don't get bothered much with this, but there are those who absolutely get enraged with this practice. Some people would venture to say that children would get the languages mixed up – not so! Your brain operates in such a manner that the thought processes within the mind of a bilingual person distinctly separate the language patterns before words are uttered. There is a mechanism that interrupts this thought process when in the middle of a sentence, a Spanish word may substitute the English word needed and cause the bilingual speaker to use that most commonly used word in place of the word intended. The word has the same meaning but just in another language. Sometimes I hear it called Spanglish! There's that word again! (I learned recently that a university in South Texas is offering a course called "Spanglish") I want to look into that someday, as languages fascinate me! I'm still to this day astounded as to why some people in this day and age are still so opposed to the idea of being bilingual. In defense of those persons not objecting to the learning and acquisition of two languages, there are many who have come to believe and understand that being bilingual is a good thing. I have learned from many of these people that they once objected to the speaking of a "foreign" language that they now encourage their children and grandchildren to acquire another language. I have friends in a nearby city that have enrolled their child in a school that is teaching him in a totally Spanish speaking setting so as to allow their child to have acquisition and mastery in two languages. They have come full circle in understanding that it's a small world thanks to technology and that we are needing to be able to communicate with others in other parts of the world. Studying a third language has been quite fascinating to me as well. I have found so many interesting avenues of study of other cultures that I have started trying to learn a fourth language and why not? I see so many foreigners that know and are fluent in five or six languages. I don't believe that their IQs are any higher than ours, as Americans, so if they can do it, so can we!

It's always humorous to me how some people will say "I can speak Spanish," and I will say, "Really? What can you say?"

They will say such things as I can say "hola", "adios", "taco", and "enchilada."

I think to myself, *What if I could only say "hi", "bye", "sandwich", and "hamburger" in English!* How lost I would have felt in my years of teaching Spanish, French, and ESL (English as a second language). I remember how funny it was for me to hear politicians on television or radio say, "If you're going to live in America you need to speak American". It sounded ridiculous to me (and still does) when someone makes an ignorant statement such as this.

I want to tell them "American" is not a language. Or if they say, if you want to speak "Mexican" go back to Mexico. I just laugh and let it slide. For some individuals, immersion into another language is the best solution to becoming bilingual. Some individuals function well by having had to speak two languages at home such as we were. Learning a third language doesn't create such an obstacle and I have often found (in my advanced English classes) that when I am uncertain as to which vowel to use to spell an English work, I translate that word to Spanish and the Spanish language automatically gives me the vowel to use as in Spanish five vowels make five sounds and five sounds only not twenty-one as in English.

5 My research paper in college to complete my master's degree included studies of children's language acquisition and how it functions in a monolingual child as opposed to a bilingual child. I studied language patterns of eighteen monolingual children and eighteen bilingual children to prove that being bilingual is not something that is an obstacle in learning basic and advanced concepts. With the permission of my supervising principal in the school where I was teaching, I was able to interview these children and their parents. I was able to apply certain learning models to both sets of children. Not all the monolingual students in this study were Anglo. Some were Hispanic and some were Black as well. Some of these children came from a bilingual home where both or one parent was fluent in either language. Some of these children came from monolingual English-speaking homes and some came from bilingual speaking homes. I am grateful that Dr. Maria Rivas, head of the education department at Texas Tech in

the eighties in Lubbock, Texas, allowed me to take a group of these children to give a demonstration of how a child can acquire a second language without his/her first language being a barrier. This method is the total physical response which I learned at East Texas State University. The method was introduced by Dr. James J. Asher where he taught at the university level in California. This method has been a life saver for me in my many years of teaching ESL, Spanish, and French at the elementary and secondary levels as well as at the university level. At the university level, I was teaching a graduate course in language acquisition for teachers at West Texas State University, who were seeking their bilingual or ESL endorsement. I am grateful that I became trilingual by choice. I remember some of my Hispanic peers trying their best to lose their bilingualism because they couldn't stand the pressure and their inability to handle and overcome being shamed, bullied and harassed for speaking a "foreign" language. They began to associate being bilingual to being ignorant or backward. I still have trouble understanding that mindset. Once again, I was re-assured that prejudice was and is a learned behavior. Children in their innocence are accepting of their peers regardless of their color or ability to speak another language, but quickly learn that there are differences in the way people from all walks of life and ethnic groups see one another. I am not a psychologist but I have learned by observation as to how a parent modeling a certain be-havior can cause a child to pick up on that and do the same. I re-cently saw a commercial on television where two young boys (one

Black, one white) were trying to fool their teacher by pretending to be one another. Just because they wore identical outfits, they thought they could fool their teacher, totally oblivious to the fact that one of them was Black and the other white. Oh, from the mouths of babes! One but rather crude observations in Spanish is a saying, "Los ninos y los borrachos no dicen mentiras." Children and drunks tell no stories!

So many sayings, proverbs, jokes, and endearments cannot be translated, they lose their meaning, flavor, or punch in another language. I remember my brothers using regionalisms when I was growing up. Being the youngest of five has definite advantages, but are quickly squashed by the disadvantages. One of those advantages is having great parental support. A definite disadvantage is that your older siblings think they can boss you around and blame the "spoiled baby" because parents tend to believe the older, wiser siblings. Another disadvantage of being the youngest is that by the time you come around your parents have already gone through the great adventures of the first tooth, the first step, the first word and so on. In Hispanic culture, it is very common for the oldest male to have the say of what goes on in the absence of the parents, even if the eldest sibling is a girl. My oldest brother ruled the roost when my parents were not there. My parents would say, "While we're gone, your brother is in charge – no questions asked" (within reason of course). Respect to older siblings as well as other adults, relatives, and especially grandparents and or great grandparents was a must. When we entered the presence of guests in our house or elsewhere, a hearty handshake was commonplace. Many Hispanic families were the huggers, kissers, or hand shakers. Families did one or all three of these gestures. In my family we were hand shakers, but we spoke to anyone we met even on the street or waved to a passerby in a car. Going around shaking people's hands was customary. Speaking to everyone was also the thing to do. Our parents taught us that it was common courtesy to acknowledge everyone. Elderly folks are held in high esteem for the values and traditions that they model. They don't have to be the most educated or in positions of high visibility to the general public, but because of the wisdom they bring to the table. Their wealth of experiences for having lived a long life. It doesn't matter if they are a part of the family or not. Looking up to the elderly was instilled in us from a very early age. Thus, in Hispanic families, older siblings, cousins, aunts, uncles, and particularly parents and grandparents are respected, not revered. I often told my own children and my students that in our home, the teacher (in school or in Sunday school) was next to God. We should respect them because they have had more experiences in life than we have had. As a child, I continued to see that Anglos were in the majority when it came to public school teachers. Therefore, many children came to believe that Hispanic and Black adults were not as smart as our Anglo counterparts. All we saw were white teachers, white principles, white counselors, white doctors, white nurses, white businessmen, white business-women. Perhaps it never occurred to me that maybe the opportunities for the Hispanics that I was surrounded with had not been available. I knew as a child that I was a mixture of Native American on my dad's side and Mexican-American on my mom's side. I found that native American and Hispanic culture held many of the same values, traditions, and customs.

Being from a migrant family, I experienced many things that perhaps I may not have experienced had I not been part of a migrant family. During my childhood, the draft for military service was beginning to surface. I remember my brothers had to register for selective service. I only remember a handful of Hispanics in military service. Even as a child, a nagging feeling in the back of my mind was why so many differences. There always seemed to be such antagonism toward the people being of Mexican descent. They would say things like, "bad bandits", "killers from a bad country". Some individuals still do.

Even though in the light of all the riots for justice and Black Lives Matter, people are losing their perspective and common goal mindset. They are wanting people, especially Anglos, to apologize for what their ancestors suffered many years ago. There is so much talk about "white privilege." As in any culture, there are those who feel entitled, regardless of their ethnic background. They tend to forget that our Anglos today were not the ones who owned slaves and they themselves were not part of the slaves. I personally feel that we shouldn't tear down any monuments or get rid of the national anthem. I believe many are being disrespectful not only to expect all these changes which are history to come about. We need to learn by our past and the implications of certain behaviors and move forward, not dwell on the past. We cannot change the past, but I believe we should strive to learn from our mistakes. I do not believe Anglos should apologize for being Anglo as well as Blacks and Mexican should not always be cast in negative personalities on radio, sports, and television. There are definite reasons why I feel we should not try to rewrite history, but move forward and make the future a better state in which to be. I regret that all Mexicans were seen in that light. Even on television, the Mexicans were the bad guys, the old drunks with the big sombreros looking sloppy and with unruly hair, and sporting a big ugly moustache. I hated that Mexicans were always cast in such a negative way. Lately on television, I have seen overkill in this area. Many commercials and movies now depict interracial marriages. It offends me to see sitcoms where the Black actors are always ridiculing the Anglo actors and most everyone sees this as ok. I do not feel this type of attitude or character downplay is necessary. It almost seems as though the screenwriters are trying to apologize for the previous portrayal of Black actors. My junior high years were such a blur. I rarely went anywhere after school. My years were spent along with my sister Josie, nursing my mother back to health as she had suffered a stroke which left her paralyzed on her left side. Many hours went into physical therapy for her to be able to walk again. She never faltered in her faith that the Lord would see her back on her feet and she was right.

I always remember her quoting her favorite Biblical verse, "Todo lo puedo en Cristo que me fortaleze Filipenses 4:13."

In my junior high mind, I would say to her "I can quote that verse in English. 'I can do all things through Christ who strengthens me' Philippians 4:13."

I told her that any verse she could quote in Spanish, I could quote in English! What fun we had doing that. She challenged me and I challenged her both in physical and mental awareness and alertness. Her speech was not altered by her stroke, so that much I was thankful for. She slowly came around to being able to walk. Her memory was as sharp as ever. She had an old Singer sewing machine which she tried to teach me how to sew on, but to no avail. To this day, sewing on a button is a challenge. I did learn, however, the art of embroidery. I don't do it very well but acceptable. Crocheting is another story. I couldn't even begin to crochet. My other aunts mastered the skill and so did some of their daughters, but not me. I wanted to be in choir, to go to contests, to read poetry, and to read novels. I loved books and magazines about other countries and I longed to visit other states and other countries.

Many decades later, I have been told by a host of people including some professionals that knowing a second language is advantageous in the business world. I must share this experience with you. I was once in Barcelona, Spain traveling with a group of people from a different state. One lady in particular was obviously frustrated in all the signs in Spanish (this is

Spain, remember) She told me she was in the mood for food from the United States and low and behold she spotted a Subway sandwich shop down the road and asked me if I would join her. I said, "Ok," and we entered the Subway. She got in line to order and was startled that the menu was in Spanish, the waiters spoke Spanish, and returned to the table where I was sitting and remarked in an exasperated voice, "None of those young people spoke English!" I gently reminded her that we were in "their" country and that their primary language was Spanish. One of the young waiters there knew a little English and was glad to help her! People all over the world will help us English speakers to get around in their countries and understand their customs and culture. I wish we in the USA would pay them the same courtesy! I understand the persecution of their ancestors coming to America to have freedom of speech, religion, etc., to flee persecution, but losing a language and customs seem to be quite a loss to me.

Not too long ago, a former student of mine came to town to give a presentation of a new agricultural program at West Texas A&M. She commented on how she regretted not becoming fluent in Spanish when she was young. Now as a college professor, she found it difficult not to be able to communicate in Spanish to some of her most important counterparts in Spanish speaking countries that she deals with. She told of how those individuals have to communicate with her in English. As they are bilingual and trilingual. She says she now encourages anyone she can to become fluent in another language. She has learned the value of knowing and being able to communicate in another language. How useful that German, Russian, Italian, French, Chinese, and Spanish would be now in this world where we have to communicate and do business with.

6My dad always took us to Colorado and New Mexico on vacation. My mother loved Red River, New Mexico. I loved Carlsbad Caverns, Pikes Peak, Garden of the Gods, Seven Fall, Old Santa Fe, Albuquerque's old town, and most of all the missions of New Mexico. I was always fascinated with the Spanish and Indian names of some of the towns and cities in those states. I remember asking my dad what the Spanish names were in English. I was fascinated to learn that Santa Fe means "holy faith," Cuchillo meant "knife," Granada means "pomegranate," Limon means "lemon," Santa Rosa – "Saint Rose," Capitan – "Captain," Corona – "Crown," Los Ranchos – "the ranches". Thus, my interest in cities with Spanish names began. I made it a point to find at least two towns in several states which has a Spanish name. My favorites are Los Angeles – "the Angels", San Francisco – "St. Francis". In the summer, our mother and dad would take us to the lake near Dennison, Texas. I was always afraid of the water and my mother would stay at the edge of the water with my sister Josie and me. We would build sand castles and collect shells. My dad would swim with my brothers, but I was afraid that I would drown. Once we saw a man get pulled out of the water as he was drowning and I remember how water gushed out of his mouth as others were trying to get him to breathe. That was the end of my attempts to swim.

As previously mentioned, my mother was raised in a traditional Roman Catholic Church. Her traditional structured method of worship was strong as her whole family would travel from Munday, Texas to Rhineland, Texas to attend church as there was not a Catholic church in Munday up until she married my Protestant dad in St. Joseph's Catholic Church. St. Joseph's in Rhineland, Texas is one of the most beautiful churches in the world. I have seen many beautiful churches all over the world and I am proud to say St. Joseph's Church ranks up there in beauty and uniqueness as any of those churches. As a young married couple, they moved to Ft. Worth, Texas to start their married life. They decided that it would be in the best interest of the family to worship in one church. My dad invited my mom to help him raise their family in unity. My mother wanting to be united agreed therefore; we were raised Protestant. A few years later, they returned to Munday to start a family. All five of us were born at home in Munday, TX with the assistance of a midwife.

7 While attending high school in Tulia, I had many experiences which have been good learning tools that have helped me navigate through life. My high school days were full of activities and new adventures. I remember my freshman year was full of sheer sadness for me. School started in September and two weeks into the school year my mother passed away. Two months into my freshman year, I found myself without a mother. I really had no enthusiasm about entering high school. My mother was gone, my brothers and older sister were married, and my sister closest in age to me was in the job corps in Guthrie, Oklahoma. I went through the motions that first year of high school. The only thing I looked forward to in school was choir. We had an outstanding seventy-two voice choir. I loved to sing. Christmas songs were my favorite. Concerts, singing at the mall during the Christmas season, contests, festivals in Enid, Oklahoma, and our choir and band concerts at school were the highlight of my freshman year in high school. I even worked up

the courage to sing a solo at contest. I didn't bring home the most talented singer at contest award, but I did get a good lesson in trying new things that are less than comfortable. In our society today, I feel we are missing the mark when it comes to dealing with losing and disappointments. Some folks even think we should give everyone an award even if it is a participation award. I do not agree with that. What a different experience singing a solo at contest was from my experience as a child singing on KTUE as a six-year-old during the Christmas season.

My homelife was lonely. My dad did his best to raise me as a single parent and I must say, he did a good job. He was strict but fair. The thing I admired the most about my dad is that he trusted me. Having his trust meant the world to me. I felt no need to lie to him. I felt no need to hide my feelings or to do illegal or immoral things. I continued to have a close relationship with my grandparents in Munday, Texas. I would get to visit them often but the missing person (my mother) left an emptiness in my life that I would have to learn to overcome gradually as I grew up. I vowed to myself that I would never break that trust that my dad had for me. I made it my mission to make my dad proud of my decisions and that I would cause him no grief. For the most part, I was able to keep my goals and walk the straight and narrow.

One of my brothers lived in Colorado, my oldest sister lived in Lamesa, Harlingen, Altus, Big Spring, wherever the Church moved them to minister in that community. My oldest brother was married and lived out in the country where he farmed with

Harold Caraway. My sister-in-law Julia was a God-send. She was a great sister-in-law. She was beautiful and talented. She could play the piano and sing. She tried to teach me both, but it didn't take. Their two children were the apple of my eye. I would go over and help them with their homework and play games with them and enjoy playing in the water with them It broke my heart when my niece and nephew talked about not being able to speak Spanish in school. Many of my childhood memories came back to haunt me as I remembered how this generation was beginning to experience what I had experienced as a youngster and what my parents had experienced as well, the feeling of non-acceptance and being pre-judged. My sister-in-law Julia came from a large family and I loved every one of her brothers and sisters (los Herrera). I loved her cousins as well (los Esparza y los Ramirez). She had many and they all lived in Tulia, so I had people who cared for me. I also had a lot of friends from school. My two best friends were Kathie Cannon (Zuniga) and Gloria Solis (Parshall) and to this day when we are now all in our late sixties, we remain good friends.

We never gave our parents too much grief. In the summers, we worked in the cotton fields. Visiting my grandparents in Munday, Texas and my brother and his kids in Colorado were the highlight of my summers. My sister Josie and I took care of my sister Isabel's kids in the summer and it was great fun. They were delightful and full of mischief. I continued to go through the motions of going to school. My cousin Andrea and I were in the same grade so we would walk to school together. My aunt and her family only lived a few blocks from us so we spent a lot of time together. We continued to go through our lives not really thinking about race, Anglo, Mexican, and Black. We were too busy living life and enjoying life to worry about racism.

In high school, I made friends easily. I had friends of every nationality. I had been fortunate to be able to make friends quickly at any age. I credit that skill to my dad who never met a stranger. I got along with everyone in general. I don't remember having enemies, but I do remember two persons in high school that loved to give all Hispanics and Blacks a hard time. We never got into fist fights or anything of the sort, but we did pull some playful pranks on those two individuals. The pranks were not designed to injure them or to get them in trouble, but they were enough to get our message across that prejudice and racism would not be tolerated. It never came to anything serious, we just kind of stayed away from people who wanted to pull the race card on us, humiliate us, belittle us (Hispanics and Blacks). I resented the fact that in order to be "accepted "by some of the Anglos, Hispanics and Blacks had to excel in some area of sports or academics. I never felt the need to be accepted the by students of other nationalities.

The majority of Anglos at Tulia High School were not racist. I wish I could say the same for their parents. A few teachers gave me an uneasy feeling. A feeling that either not much was expected of Hispanics and Blacks to the feeling that we were expected to go above and beyond to gain their approval. Most Hispanics and Blacks bent over backwards to be accepted by our teachers. After all, our parents expected us to be respectful, to be cooperative, and most of all to not cause any trouble for the adults in the school system. We experienced more pre-judgement from adults than from my own peers. Once again confirmed that prejudice and racism are learned and modeled by adults. My friend Kathie is the most non-judgmental person I know. If she was ever told anything about hanging around Mexicans, I would always hear her say, "What's wrong with having friends of all races? We are all people, we are all the same." I always admired her for not pre-judging people. She loved people for what they stood for and not for the color of their skin. She is a true example of what it means to love people regardless of their ethnic background, their religious beliefs, and the color of their skin. Later in life, Kathie became a nurse. A great profession with persons of her character and compassion.

Through the years, I have made many friends who were not prejudiced but came from families that were. This prejudice is not limited to Anglos, Mexicans, or Blacks or any other ethnic groups. There is division among Anglo families as well. Some families were not accepted by other Anglos and the same is true in Mexican and Black families. I have continued to see this division and non-acceptance among same ethnic groups. It is not difficult to see these differences in a small town. Some Anglos do not include other Anglos that are not in their same socio-economic levels are therefore excluded from joining certain groups in the community. There continues to this day, a division not only of different colors of skins but in socio-economic status as well. There continues to be divisions all over the world, the poor, the working class, the elites. It is mind boggling how many divisions there are among human beings in any part of the world in any country. Divisions continue to exist among the Protestant, Catholic, Jews, Muslims, etc. Even though many of us are Christian, there is still a division in manner of worship and beliefs. Racism still exists in this day and age. There seems to be somewhat tolerance to the differences that separate us. It is a learned behavior in any group. Children learn what they see and live by example. It is true when you hear that children learn by what they live. It is disheartening to see people from different ethnic groups behave in a way that demonstrated that they are ashamed of their ethnicity. For a child to behave as if he/she is better than others is a learned behavior. They picked it up somewhere. They were not born prejudiced but learned at a very early age to mimic the behavior of their immediate caretakers. They take up the attitudes of the ones that raise them. Some are fortunate to grow up in a non-judgmental environment and other are very unfortunate to grow up in an environment where prejudice is alive and well and impose their beliefs and actions upon innocent children who are little sponges, who soak up information from their environment.

I always noticed that different ethnic groups kept to themselves in their compartmentalized groups. We were no exception. We were surrounded by Mexicans. Anglos were surrounded by Anglos and Blacks were surrounded by Blacks. There were instances where there was a mixture in certain activities but it was rare to see dating among the different ethnic groups. Persons who dated out of their ethnic group were at times given a hard time by their families and by others, so it was uncommon to see this mixture. Everyone in my immediate family married within the same ethnic group, but that has not been the case with the younger generations. Even though the supreme court ruled that it was legal for persons to marry outside their race, I knew very little of this ruling even though I was a sophomore in high school. It could be that perhaps I was never aware that marrying someone of a different race was unconstitutional. We could learn a good lesson from the younger generations who have broken this barrier. Most of them look for a partner with which to share their life on the basis of their character and love and not worry too much about the ethnic group they belong to. I do have room to talk about this as I have a mixture of Anglo and Black in my family. In my extended family, I also have Oriental cousins! Some of our older generations when questioned about this, would tell us that it was not so much to separate us from other ethnic groups but to protect us from the criticism, the hardships of marrying and raising a family of diverse ethnic groups. One of the main hardships that I often saw within a marriage of persons of different ethnic groups was that they were shunned by both groups. The children of those marriages suffered because of the non-acceptance of either group. Persons in my generation chose to not teach their children Spanish because they didn't want their children to suffer the same humiliation that we had suffered. Years later, this same generation could kick themselves for not granting their children the opportunity to become bilingual. They found out that "it's ok" to speak and understand more than one language. There were differences that had nothing to do with the color of the skin, but of different "costumbres" (customs) beliefs and ways of life that were so different. I do remember suffering some ridicule over some of our beliefs in certain things such as cures for certain illnesses and traditions we practiced where our grandparents were instrumental in instilling in us. I remember being told that some of the remedies we practiced were nothing short of witchcraft which I knew was totally false but suffered ridicule over them nevertheless. In later years, I remember these same folk remedies being practiced by other ethnic groups and being accepted. Some years later I became interested in folk remedies and also was intrigued by Negro folk remedies.

It was in high school, that I became interested in learning a third language. I enrolled in French class at THS with Mr. Flanagan. I enjoyed learning this third language and found the speech patterns very similar to those of Spanish. Knowing Spanish was such an advantage in my acquisition of French. I would practice my French with my sister who was a good sport and let me try new phrases on her while she tried to guess the meaning. She was pretty good at guessing the meaning as she was very fluent in Spanish as well. I did a lot of digging into the French language and culture which helped me in later years as a French teacher and later traveling with my students to France. As there were no other French speaking adults in my immediate surroundings, I read many French historical novels and much later read French literature to my infant daughter which put her right to sleep!

The summer between my junior and senior years at THS, my family and I suffered a very serious accident about five miles south of town by the Eunice Elevators, we were turning left and a big semi-truck struck the back of our car and made it spin and turn over. All five of us in the car were seriously injured. My dad, who was driving, hurt his stomach and intestines with the steering wheel. My sister had forty-five stitches on her head as she suffered a cut from the windshield. I was crushed between the back seat and the front seat with a broken knee, a broken hip, and all my ribs were broken as well. My five-year-old niece broke her leg in two places and lost her baby teeth. My eight-year-old niece was killed in that accident. I remember the lights of the ambulance as they carried my niece to the hospital. It was noon but I felt like it was dusk. I remember the jaws of life being used to open the car doors. I distinctly heard a voice which I recognized saying, "Are you ok? Can you hear me?" That familiar voice was that of E. W. Riley. He had stopped on his way back from Plainview when he saw the accident. The next thing I remember was the X-ray technician telling me to lie still on the X-ray table. This was June fifth, so we spent many weeks in the hospital, but was out the week school started right after Labor Day. That was the way my senior year in high school started.

My senior year was memorable. I loved all my teachers and my classes. I loved the Tulia Hornets and had a blast being in the pep squad. We took a bus with pep squad members and three buses with band students and instruments. We made a lot of noise and traveled far on those Friday nights. I remember playing in Seminole, Dumas, Childress but my favorite was when we played the Dimmitt Bobcats! What rivalry that exists to this day!

The only bad memory of my senior year in high school was when a counselor told me that I shouldn't even think about going to college.

She said, "Your dad will never be able to afford to send you to college, besides, you are not college material."

Those words stuck in my mind. I had never been disrespectful to any adult let alone an educator but I remember telling her, "You just wait and see. I will go to college. I will become a teacher and I will be back to talk to you."

Many years passed and I did have a chance to talk to her again. She had retired and was subbing when I met her in the teacher's lounge. I introduced myself to her, as I know she did not remember me. I told her that I was happy to see her doing well and that I wanted to let her know that I had finished college at West Texas State University with a BA in Education with a kindergarten endorsement, an ESL endorsement and a bilingual endorsement. I had earned a masters of education and all level Spanish and French from East Texas State University. She was very cordial to me and told me she was proud of me. I didn't have the heart to tell her that her words had been my inspiration to continue my education. Sometimes it's those harsh words from someone that cause us to have the energy and drive to carry on.

8 While working to finish my degree at West Texas State University in Canyon, I married my high school sweetheart from Flomot, Texas, a small community in Motley County sixty miles southeast of Tulia. My husband went to school in a tiny town where K-12 was in the same building. He too is bilingual and that is about the extent of similarities that we share. He is the oldest of five children, I am the youngest of five children. He was Catholic and I was Protestant. He was at Clarendon College when I was at Amarillo College and WT. He wore Levi's, boots and a hat, I had never worn boots or jeans or a hat in my life. He loves action movies and I like romantic comedies. He loved fast cars and I was satisfied with an old '65 Rambler that I drove. He was from a farming community where he grew up first through twelfth grade. I was from a migrant family. He was fan of the rodeo and I had never been to one. He loved country and western music and I loved Spanish music. He loved Bob Wills and Willie Nelson, I loved

Jose Alfredo Jimenez and Little Joe y la Familia. He loved to dance waltzes and cowboy two steps, I loved to dance rancheras and polkas. I love to travel and he is a homebody. So, as you can see, he had a lot to learn!

I started my teaching career in Kress, Texas after having been a teacher's assistant in Tulia and Valley School (Turkey and Quitaque) ISD. I taught kindergarten through eighth grade migrant students in Kress. Many of my childhood memories came to me as I did my best to give these children the best school experience they could have. I remember belonging to a migrant family as a child and I longed for them to love to read and to learn. They too wanted to gather and grasp as much material possible before they moved on to other communities. My heart broke as I watched them being ridiculed by young and old because of their transient status in the community. I did my best to reassure them that they were loved by the staff and the other children. Many of the parents confided in me that they were happy to see a Hispanic teacher for their children. At last, they could talk to someone who understood their plight in life. Some of those migrant families became permanent residents of that small-town others left and never looked back.

The following year, I was hired as a bilingual second grade teacher in Tulia. I lived in Tulia so I really was excited to get a teaching job there, even though a piece of my heart stayed in Kress. My immediate supervisor, Mr. Bill Hicks, was a caring, compassionate individual who genuinely cared about the welfare and education of all the students. At that time, the elementary school was called East Ward. I always wondered why the schools were called East Ward, Central Ward, North Ward, etc. It had always been that way, even when I was a first grader at East Ward. It wasn't until years later when the name was changed to W.V. Swinburn after an outstanding educator and superintendent in Tulia, Swisher County, Texas. Mr. Swinburn was instrumental in many of the advances of the education at Tulia independent school district. He was truly deserving to have a school named in honor of him. Some of the Swinburn family still resides in Tulia. I taught one of his grandsons in second grade a few years later. My eight and a half years at East Ward as a second grade teacher brought many rewards as well as disappointments in human beings in general. I learned that being one of two Hispanic teachers in the entire TISD faculty was a challenge. There were other Hispanic employees at TISD but only in the cafeteria, as custodians, or teacher assistants. I felt the sting when I was looked down on, excluded from little circles of cliques in the entire school system. I was not only excluded by my Anglo co-teachers, but from the other Hispanics that worked for the system. I have to make it totally clear at this point that not all Anglos and not all Hispanics were guilty of this. Even within Anglo and Hispanic circles, people with degrees were sometimes ridiculed by their own ethnic groups. I would often hear people that had not earned a degree talk about people that had earned a degree as "smarty pants" and sometimes would say things like, "That little piece of paper (degree) doesn't make them better or smarter." I will never apologize for having a bachelor's degree or a master's degree. I feel like I earned them and I will continue to be proud of that fact. I will never flaunt them around, but I refuse to apologize for having earned them. There were those that were totally accepting of me as a degreed teacher in the system. They didn't treat me any different than they did the other Anglos or Hispanics.

One very disappointing thing early in my career as well as later on in my career up until my retirement thirty-nine years later was that some Hispanic parents were still not teaching their children Spanish. They continued to pass on the stigma of being considered lower class because they were Hispanic. During this time, the late sixties and early seventies, this division of classes, be it socio economic and ethnicity, were prevalent in this part of West Texas. Many Hispanic parents stated that they did not want their children to go through what they and their parents had gone through as a result of not being accepted. Here within lies a perfect example of learned behavior. I had experienced this non-acceptance as a child, which continued through my school years and even carried on to my college experience as a young Hispanic. We were a minor part of the population of Hispanics and Blacks at the university level. Foreign students were few at this point in time. A handful of Oriental students attended WT.

There were only a few societies that we were included in such as Alpha Chi and Kappa Delta Pi that saw Mexican-American and Blacks inducted into. They are honor societies based on grades in certain majors. I was so proud of my induction into these two honor societies that I treasure my induction certificates to this day. I learned about navigating my way through the university system as we say in Hispanic society – "a sombrerasos y cachuchasos" which has no literal translation but can be understood as by leaps and bounds, by falling on one's face and picking oneself up or as some say "flying by the seat of our pants". We had very little guidance from our advisors. Perhaps it was the advisors I happened to be assigned. Whatever the case may have been, I learned to try to figure it out! Maybe that's why I think it is important to teach students to learn to reason and problem solve. It was what pushed us through university life. I couldn't "google" the answers! The closest I had come to a computer in my college days was working on the key punch machine at Amarillo college with Dr. Irion. Some of you can relate. Those key punch machines took up nearly an entire room. Nothing like these little computers or Chromebooks that students now use.

During my years as a second grade teacher in the Tulia public schools, I learned so much about human nature. I learned so much about acceptance and rejection. Once again, I felt the sting of not being accepted for the degreed, eager teacher I was. Some of the Anglo parents talked to the principal about their reluctance of having a Hispanic teacher teach their child. I cried myself to sleep many nights, praying for guidance and the courage to go on. I vowed to myself that I would not only set a self-goal of being not only a good teacher, but an exceptional teacher. I went above and beyond in preparation for my lessons for my second graders. I wanted them to have wonderful and memorable experiences. I wanted them to love school. I worked hard to make sure that they would never experience favoritism on my part. The first year I taught second grade, I was assigned to a bilingual room. The state of Texas required that if there were twenty or more students in one grade level, the school must offer a bilingual program to serve those students. Tulia was designated as a school that must offer a bilingual classroom for each grade level that qualified. At that time, Mrs. Mary Frances Wynne taught the first grade bilingual classroom and I was assigned the second grade bilingual classroom. Later, a third grade bilingual classroom was also added to this. This made our rooms full of Hispanic children and we were in charge of helping them make the transition to English but not losing their Spanish. It was an ideal situation, the only drawback was that some Hispanic students were once again segregated from other Hispanics, Anglos, and Blacks. There was a division among parents of these children. Some felt their children were separated by ethnicity but the majority of the parents assigned to these bilingual rooms were thankful that their children would be able to function in both languages. We provided many opportunities for parental involvement.

The next few years of teaching second grade were quite different. I was assigned a classroom full of Anglos, Blacks, and Mexicans. I was told by my supervisor that I would be allowed to teach the children Spanish if their parents so desired. Many parents took advantage of this opportunity to have their children introduced to a second language. I began to see that through the guidance of Mr. Bill Hicks, parents were beginning to be accepting of their children being assigned to a bilingual classroom where Spanish would be introduced. I still had parents who wanted their child removed from my classroom because they feared that having a Hispanic teacher would be detrimental to the education of their child. I had the experience of having conferences with parents because they were not sure they wanted their child in my room. I had to prove that I could actually speak English well! How humiliating was that? Determined not to let them come between my love of teaching and humanity in general, I carried on. Every year I would have those parents who questioned my ability to teach their children. Every year I knew that I was to face prejudice and pre-judgement in my abilities to be their precious child's teacher. It was tolerable because I knew I had the support of a great principal and superintendent that believed in me. I carried on determined to make my second grade class the best class those children would ever have. I took an enormous amount of time in preparation for my classes. I was determined to teach to every learning style. I had students with very high IQs and children with learning disabilities, children who were bilingual and monolingual, children who came from wealthy families and children from dirt poor families, children on free lunches, children who wore designer clothes and those who had to wait to get to school for the school nurse to find them something to wear. I had respectful children and disrespectful children. I had children who were visual or auditory learners as well as those who had to move about and touch everything. No social distancing was practiced there! At that time, we were assigned a teacher with whom we were to partner with as we were to teach all nine subjects to our self-contained classroom.

Mrs. Shelly Borchardt Dunn and I were team teachers for four years. She always said, "If you can teach them to throw a football. I can teach them to sing." Yes, we taught P.E. and music as well! We had great fun with our students and we got to know them and their families well. We not only taught the three Rs but had the opportunity to put on programs and plays for the parents. We had contests in our classes. We played and learned vocabulary and math facts with flashcards. The children learned and got to move around and be competitive. We taught them to win and to lose. We taught them not only to take pride in winning, but to learn to lose gracefully and strive to improve. We were preparing them to live in a competitive world where you win some and lose some and to deal with the rewards and consequences that come with competition. Not everyone received a winning ribbon or a participation certificate, but everyone received the encouragement to carry on, to strive to excel, and to move forward. We were teaching them that this is a competitive world we live in and that we have to learn to do our very best.

9 It was during those years as a second grade teacher that my husband and I adopted our two daughters. One in 1978 and one in 1979. They made our family complete. Now that they are grown and live in different states of the country, we have learned to cherish the precious little time we spend with them as adults. Experiences with them is another book, not dealing with prejudice and racism. The only comment I will make is that in our own families there were those certain individuals who did not accept these "adopted" children as "real" relatives. So, we suffered the sting of division within our own family as well as some other families in the community. Again, a learned behavior. I had to cling to the grace that we are afforded by the Almighty that we are "adopted children of God".

In the mid-eighties, I was assigned to teach Spanish, French, and ESL at the high school level. My first reaction was, "NO!" I didn't sign up to teach that age group. Besides that, I loved my second graders. I wanted to stay where the love of learning still shone in those children's eyes, where every day was an adventure full of discovery and amazement. To go on our field trips out to Lake Mackenzie where Mr. Davey would show us the bat caves and the wild flowers, the anticipation of Christmas parties with pinatas and Valentine cards with special messages and Easter egg hunts with our mothers and baby siblings along. Every year I became so attached to the children and to their families, learning about everyday life, customs, and traditions that made us such a diverse community. I had become comfortable and felt accepted after those first few challenging years. But I had to accept change and learn to face new challenges. I feel the Lord has other plans for our lives when we are at a point when we become to feel complacent that He challenges us look beyond our safe and secure world. As a child, I had felt safe and secure in the safety net of a good Christian home. I had to accept the challenge and move forward.

10

I began my secondary teaching career in the middle of the year. A new teacher had been hired to take my place in second grade. I am forever grateful to Mrs. Elaine Bevill who took the time to come get to know my students before I left them at mid-term. I have to admit that it was one of the hardest things I have ever had to experience. Parting with that age group broke my heart. I cried myself to sleep many a night, worrying about how I was going to meet this new challenge. Was I going to have to go through the same experience again of not being accepted because of my ethnicity? Would I be challenged again as to whether I would be accepted by this new age group and their parents and the new faculty, I would have to get used to coming in at the beginning of a new semester? How would I deal with the age difference, the teaching techniques, the new subject matter, the new rules and regulations about contact with the children? I came from a happy place where I could hug the children and sit them in my lap to comfort them in time of distress or uncertainty to a place where I had to learn to keep my distance, to deal with problems in a totally new way.

Before going into the new semester in a new campus with a new faculty, new students, and a whole new set of challenges, I had the Christmas holidays to prepare. It was during the holidays that I came down with pneumonia and lost my father to heart failure. It was a dark time in my life, but I feel that the Lord was really putting me to the test. I went in to my new position with a strong determination to do well. I made up my mind that nothing would deter me from being the strong and caring teacher that I had been those last nine years of my teaching career. I had to get used to a totally new different way of managing my time. I no longer had the self-contained classroom with twenty-six smiling, eager to learn faces who saw no fault in me. I was now faced with twenty-four different faces and personalities every forty-five minutes, each who came with their own agendas and strong personalities and attitudes. I knew I could count on the support of my new supervising principal, Mrs. Linda Hicks. She was totally different from Mr. Bill Hicks who had been my supervisor for the previous eight and a half years. They were different in their approach of education. However, they were equally supportive of their staff and genuine interest in the love for the students and their varying abilities and personalities.

Dealing with a new curriculum, a new campus, and a new age group was extremely challenging to say the least. I had students who immediately accepted me and wanted to learn and were genuinely interested in the subject matter. Then there were those who resented being assigned a new teacher with a whole new different teaching style than their previous teacher in the middle of the school year. Both types of students were a true challenge. A small group of students were determined to make my life miserable and weren't shy about the things they did and said. They were aggressively rude and disrespectful and their parents were unhappy as well. Once again, I felt the sting of prejudice and non-acceptance. Once more I dealt with the need to prove that I was quite capable of teaching the material I was expected to teach. It took all the strength and will-power I could gain from within myself to not let these few rude and disrespectful students get me down. It wasn't only the Anglo students that made up this little group, but some were Hispanic and some were Black. Many of their parents had told them not to take any bull from a "Mexican teacher". I went through the conferences again with this principal to assure the parents that I was ok to teach their child, I did indeed speak proper English, and that I was a college graduate, that I was an experienced teacher, and that I would do all I could to make their child's learning experience a good one. They majority of the faculty accepted me as their teaching peer. There were a few who still were not quite sure how to take me. The only thing that impressed them was that I was trilingual, but that was about the extent of it. It was daunting to me how in this same building – Tulia High School, sixteen years later I was on the other side of the table. In the seventies as a student who was ridiculed and punished for speaking Spanish to the eighties where I was now a teacher of that language I was forbidden to speak and another foreign language to boot! What turns life takes!

My teaching methods differed with the difference in age of the students, but I still felt compelled to teach to all the learning styles. These kids were just "kids" like my second graders, only bigger and older. They stilled yearned to go beyond the lecture and note taking style of learning. I found that I still had those type of students who needed to hear, to write, to learn visually, to move around, to touch, to feel objects that caused them to acquire a language. There was much laughter, not ridicule, in the many ways of articulating and pronouncing words. They took joy in comparing the differences and similarities in the languages. They loved flashcards and contests, going to the board and writing words and sentences. The enjoyed preparing poetry, prose, spelling, and plays for their contests at South Plains college as well as in the classroom. They loved learning about the other cultures by going to the cultural center at Texas Tech's cultural center, the Buddy Holly museum and especially the Mexican bakery in downtown Lubbock who catered to them during the "Day of The Dead" feast. Through the years, the parents of these students became accepting of their child's love of learning a different language. It took the adults much longer than it did the students. Many of their parents were products of the generations where speaking another language was taboo. They wanted to protect their children from the injustices they suffered at the hands of a few who felt the need to exclude them, to ridicule them and to make them feel less human. What a sad existence that must be!

That first year of teaching at the high school level brought many joys and disappointments. One surprise that my supervisor had for me that semester was that I was to be a junior class sponsor and that because I had replaced a certain teacher, I was now head junior class sponsor in charge of the junior-senior prom, which was to take place in early April. Once again I felt the sting of prejudice from parents who were unaccepting and angry that not only did they have a new junior sponsor, but a" Mexican" to boot. Some were not very nice and pretty vocal about that situation, but with the help of the other dedicated junior sponsors and the students, we were able to pull off a beautiful and memorable prom. Needless to say, I became accustomed to challenges that were thrown my way. Working with a caring staff, I was able to enjoy the next twenty-eight years. I learned to enjoy and challenge my students regardless of their attitudes and willingness or unwillingness to work. We crossed may obstacles in the area of learning, but we learned to tackle them and have a good time while doing it. Ten of those twenty-eight years, I also took on the task of cheerleader sponsor. That was a whole new kind of challenge. The groups differed from year to year, but I had to learn that their different personalities and good qualities make them the individuals they are today. For ten years I had the pleasure of working with these young ladies and their parents. It took the parents longer to accept me. I had learned to take on these challenges by now!

The last five years of this challenge was eased by Mrs. Sheila Via, who came onboard to help with the junior varsity squad. We worked well together and I appreciated her tolerance and her bookkeeping skills!

For a few years, I had been thinking about how wonderful it would be to be able to travel to another country with my students. I thought about how great it would be to have them experience another culture first hand. I worked up the courage to ask our then superintendent Mr. Mike Vineyard about this possibility. He presented my idea to the school board and they ruled favorably. I held and introductory meeting of students and parents who might be interested in this venture. Several students and parents responded. We made plans to take the students to Mexico. (Mexico City, Taxco, a mining city in the state of Guerrero and to the beautiful beaches in Acapulco). These trips to Mexico and to Europe (the first being London, Paris, and Rome) became quite popular with the Spanish and French classes. There were guidelines to being able to go on these trips. First of all, the students must have been enrolled in a foreign language for two years. They had to raise their own money and yes, their parents were invited to go on these trips. Many parents accompanied us on these trips. It was my dream, for students at Tulia High School to know that there was life beyond Tulia, Swisher County, Texas. I wanted them to experience another culture, another country that spoke a language other than English as their primary language. I now knew that if a parent trusted me with their child in another country, they had complete faith in my ability to teach their child. Many trips followed that, sixteen more to different parts of Mexico, in Europe, London, France, Italy, Switzerland, and many more, and in the South Pacific, Australia, New Zealand, Tahiti, and in the United States, New York and Washington DC. I believe that a good education begins at home but we can have a richer, more meaningful experience in the way of travel. I was glad that the parents of these students that traveled with me entrusted their care to me and other sponsors. Many years after these students traveled, many have returned to these countries on their own or as a university experience. They are no longer afraid of the unknown, the fear of experiencing another culture has turned into pure joy of having had the opportunity to visit another country in their young lives. Years later, some of these young adults have written me letters, postcards and most recently texts about their experiences in another country and how grateful they are not to be afraid to open themselves to the experiences that life affords them.

After my retirement from teaching, I went to work for the sister company of the student travel company to the adult travel division. A group of adults await with me to be able to travel to Israel in the very near future. Our plans were pushed back because of the Covid-19 pandemic.

11

One of the darkest days of my adult life was in late April of 2019, when I was served with a trespass warning of the house where my oldest sister resided. I was not allowed to visit my sister for five and a half months. Neither my sister nor I or her youngest daughter were allowed to visit her. We were told that it was for her protection. I never quite knew or understood why she needed protection from us, her sisters or her daughter. She and I had traveled the world over, London, Paris, Rome, Mexico City. We traveled in the United States from California on the west coast to Virginia on the east coast, and suddenly she needed protection. Go figure. She went to her heavenly Father in the early hours of one Thursday morning in early January, alone, in her protective room. The consolation that I have to this day is that she loved me and knew that I loved her in spite of our forced separation. She was a Christian that loved the Lord and was faithful till the end of her days here on earth. She served her Lord and Master till her dying day.

Her church family's visits were few and far between, but they too continued to love her and pray for her. Next to my parents, my siblings were and are the closest persons to my heart, having lost my mother at the age of fourteen and my father at the age of thirty-six, my oldest brother at the age of twenty-six, I felt extremely blessed to still have my oldest sister, my other sister that was only two and a half years older than me, and my brother who is eight years older than me. My two sisters were my best friends. We traveled together, spent holidays together, celebrated birthdays, attended bi-annual family reunions together, got manicures and pedicures together, and shared our deepest secrets. The respect I had for my sisters was beyond measure. I talk about this in the past tense because in January of 2020, I lost my oldest sister, then three months later in April of 2020, I lost my other sister. Seven months later, on my birthday, November 28th 2020, I lost my life's partner, my husband of forty-nine years and ten months. He lost his life at Rose Medical Center in Denver because of Covid-19. A few weeks later, I lost four more precious friends to this dreadful virus. For months after their passing, I found myself in a state of disbelief. How could I have lost my two best friends. my husband, three comadres and one of my comadre's son in a period of eleven months? I was inconsolable. I cried at the mere mention of their name, a picture, a memory that we shared. Even though my relationship with each of them was different, there were so many similarities in our relationships that even I was astounded in remembering. I drowned my thoughts of sorrow in tears and only found refuge in my relationship with God.

Many things changed after the death of my two sisters, my husband and my friends. I felt and continue to feel a sense of loss that is beyond explanation. Friends and family have helped me through this grieving process but others have turned away from the closeness we once shared. I don't know if it is because they don't know what to say or because others are pulling them farther away from a relationship that we once shared. Grieving has taught me that many times we are alone in our sadness. Only God can fill the void left by such great losses. I understand that we all have different ways of grieving but I know I will continue to reach out to my family in spite of some of their voluntary separation.

Years ago, I had returned to my roots of the religion of my mother (Roman Catholic). I found peace and comfort in the Mass, the Holy Eucharist, and the Rosary. It was during this first quarter of the year 2020 that the world came to a screeching halt because of the pandemic of the coronavirus. It was in the middle of March that we found ourselves having to shelter-in-place, do social distancing, and wear masks to protect ourselves and others from spreading this disease. The media became engulfed in updates about active cases, recoveries and deaths associated with the coronavirus. I found myself with much alone time. We were constantly reminded of the plagues of yesteryear, the Spanish Flu, Ebola, etc. We were bombarded with the laying of the blame for this outbreak. We were told by some that it was political, that all of this could have been avoided if precautions would have been in place earlier. Many futurists came forward telling us that they had predicted this many years ago. I was reminded of a novel I read in high school by George Orwell called *1984*. I read this book in 1968 and a few years later *1984* came to be and it was shockingly accurate. Many people say they can predict the future and say that scientifically, certain things can be proven or disproven. I may be old school, but I still believe that only God knows the future. After all, he holds the future. I wasn't until my adult life that I came to understand many things that I had been taught as a child. One in particular that sticks out in my mind is TIME. I now understand that our time is not God's time. Time isn't measured the same by human beings and God. There are so many theories about what is going to happen in the near future. Questions being asked are: Will an effective vaccine be available to help with the coronavirus? Will the economy recover? Will schools, churches and business reopen? When will things be back to normal? Somethings I have seen happen in society today is that parents are spending much more time with their families (home-schooling) takes on a whole new meaning. I see education and educators being so much more appreciated. I remember people saying – "Teachers don't do much" well, I now see a much deeper appreciation for the school system from caretakers of buildings, to bus drivers, to cafeteria workers, to teachers, to aides, to school nurses, to administrators. Everyone that has any part in the education of youngsters need to be seen in a different light. I once saw a Facebook post by a frustrated mother now at home with her two children say, "I have been homeschooling my two children ages six and eight for an hour and eleven minutes and I've had it! Teachers need to be paid a billion dollars." Another humorous post said, "Teacher, you lied when you said my child was a joy to have in class!" I'm reminded of the old saying, "Until you've walked a mile in my shoes, keep your opinion and suggestions to yourself." The education system is close to my heart as I was an educator in Texas public schools for thirty-nine years and a substitute teacher for three more. Forty-two years is a long time!

The medical profession as stated before is dear to my heart, as my two sisters were nurses for many, many years. They worked in hospitals, home-health, nursing homes, and immunization clinics. I see these health professionals in the trenches amid this pandemic and I pray constantly for their health, their families, and their continued strength to continue caring for the sick and dying. It takes a very caring, strong, and committed individual to put their lives on the line daily to do the work in a profession that is their calling. Sometimes we take prayer so lightly and we throw around those words so readily, that they may become meaningless to others, but we must keep our focus on what we are praying about. My grandmother Antonia used to tell us, "If you pray, don't worry and if you worry, don't pray!" Spend your energy in prayer! I am reminded of a song we sang at Mass – "Consider the lilies, they don't toil nor mend, but there's not a king with more splendor than them. For we have a heavenly Father above, that brings out the stars, tells the sun when to shine." So, if our heavenly Father does all that, where does that leave the global warming theory?

If you can't tell by now that I am a die-hard Christian, I don't know what could convince you. I once met a young man in graduate school that asked me this daunting question, "Is there anyone or anything that could convince you that Jesus Christ is not the answer?" and I remember giving him "the look" and saying, "NEVER" and he very seriously said, "Well, there is not anyone or anything that could convince me that Allah is not the answer." I learned much that day as we were leaving our class on "The Great Religions of The World" I remember thinking how our life experiences had shaped us into the individuals that were now studying and learning to respect other cultures and their beliefs. Not to be so quick to judge the decisions of others. I couldn't condemn him for his beliefs, but I hoped and prayed that someday by the example we Christians were setting that living, others would come to know Jesus Christ. Years after my father became a widower, he remarried a woman who came with three young girls. I never lived in his new household as I was married by then. He then began a new chapter in his life, but continued to instill good values and a strong work ethic in his new family. He and his second wife had two daughters of their own. They too were charged with developing strong characters and a love for the Lord. They too are true bilinguals and proud of it.

As the election of the president of the United States approached, there were many comments and ideas bombarding the media on what we should believe and what we should discard as "fake news". During the Democratic and Republican national conventions, both sides have made some very powerful statements in troublesome issues facing America today. In particular, one statement made by one of the candidates about African-Americans being monolithic – Broken into its roots, "mono" and "lithic", monolithic simply means "one stone". When monolithic is used to describe something societal, whether it be like a religion or as organization – it has a rather negative connotation. A good example is a monolithic society or ethnic group, it regards it as a rigid and homogenous, not open to new ideas. It can be very dangerous to refer to a group of human beings as monolithic. It gives the undertone of calling a particular ethnic group as rigidly close-minded. It is literally clumping a group of people as having no individuality or the ability to think for themselves. Growing up, I remember Blacks and Hispanics were led to believe that because of their nationality and/or socio-economic status, they were encouraged/pushed into belonging to a particular political party. So many ideas were put into their head about how they must belong to that political party because it was in the interest of the "poor" man. They learned about that particular party's belief by word of mouth and lived in fear of losing their jobs or homes. Many of Blacks and Hispanics fell in this trap. So much progress has been made in educating the entire population, so that people can know that they have a voice, a vote and an opinion that is valid. My father was one of those Hispanics that became affiliated with a certain political party. His loyalty and sense of belonging was overwhelming. Regardless of platform changes, he remained steadfast and loyal to that political party. It wasn't until years later that he saw that the political party that he was affiliated with and loyal to, had some ideas and ideals that were contrary to his inner beliefs and he began to study the issues and the candidates who presented these varying views. It was then that I began to see my dad open his eyes to the reality of suppressed ideas and narrow-minded thoughts being presented to the general public as Gospel.

To this day, my adult family members go above and beyond looking at the issues and making their own choices when it comes to political agendas. The 2020 conventions have really touched on immigration – we have to recognize that at some point, we are all immigrants. We have come full circle to help everyone understand that we all (our ancestors) came to this country for many reasons, be they political, economical, or freedom of religion. Racism and prejudice come in every form. In listening to the First Lady speak, people started tweeting and posting on Facebook, "That woman can't even speak English"; "Her accent is awful". I personally took offence to these comments as I know I have an accent that some people still ridicule me or my family members that don't speak perfect English, but I have learned not to let it get to me or define me. I am proud to be trilingual. I am proud that I can communicate with people in many countries. I am proud of that skill. I have never apologized for being trilingual. My parents and grandparents were bilingual and proud of it. They felt more comfortable communicating in their first language. I feel very confident in speaking two of my three languages. My third language is not as fluent but believe me, I can make myself understood in my third language. All multi-lingual speakers are more comfortable in their dominant language. As we anticipated the election of our president in November 2020, we must be mindful of all the rhetoric making the rounds in our world. We have to continue to pray for this nation. We are indeed blessed to live in this country. It is not the country that is racist and prejudice. It is the people with narrow-minded beliefs and the idea that it is their way or the highway that cause us to be labeled. There is no one that can change my mind about the mercy of God Almighty. As in the Gospel of (Luke 12:48) To whom much is given, much is required. If you have heard that line of wisdom, you know it means we are held responsible for what we have. If we have been blessed with talents, wealth, knowledge, time and the like, it is expected to benefit others. We have been graced with theological virtues of faith, hope, and love (charity). We have been gifted with the cardinal values of prudence, temperance, justice, and fortitude. We have been graced with gifts of the Holy Spirit being wisdom, understanding, right judgement (counsel), courage, knowledge, reverence (piety), wonder, and awe (fear of the Lord). We have also been gifted with the fruits of the Holy Spirit which are charity, joy peace, patience, goodness, mildness, faith, modesty, continency, and chastity. We as a nation have been given much and we are expected to welcome the refugee, not to count the cost, because as confirmed Christians we are called to called to perform the spiritual works of mercy, to warn the sinner, instruct the ignorant, to counsel the doubtful, to comfort the sorrowing, to bear wrongs patiently, to forgive all injuries, and to pray for the living and the dead. We are also instructed to perform the corporal works of mercy given to us by the Holy Spirit, to feed the hungry, to give drink to the thirsty, to clothe the naked, to visit the sick, to shelter the homeless, to visit the imprisoned, and to bury the dead. So, as you can see, we are indeed a gifted nation. We must never forget that and become complacent. So, are we up to the challenge? Will we continue to be negative models for all future generations. Will we continue to be accepting of racism and prejudice? We as free-willed individuals need to set the standard to treat everyone with respect! May our faith and fear become faith over fear!